A Room Full of Shadows

A Room Full of Shadows

RONALD L. FAUST

RESOURCE *Publications* • Eugene, Oregon

A ROOM FULL OF SHADOWS

Copyright © 2019 Ronald L. Faust. All rights reserved. Except for brief quotations in critical publications or reviews, no part of this book may be reproduced in any manner without prior written permission from the publisher. Write: Permissions, Wipf and Stock Publishers, 199 W. 8th Ave., Suite 3, Eugene, OR 97401.

Resource Publications
An Imprint of Wipf and Stock Publishers
199 W. 8th Ave., Suite 3
Eugene, OR 97401

www.wipfandstock.com

PAPERBACK ISBN: 978-1-5326-7867-7
HARDCOVER ISBN: 978-1-5326-7868-4
EBOOK ISBN: 978-1-5326-7869-1

Manufactured in the U.S.A.   APRIL 8, 2019

Dedicated to

K
and
Ruthann Shetler

"A small body of determined spirits fired by an unquenchable faith in their mission can alter the course of history."

—Mahatma Gandhi

Contents

Preface | ix
Acknowledgements | xi

QUADRANT I | 1
    InsignificANT | 3
    Taxing | 6
    Jobs | 14
    Games | 18
    Peace | 22
    Honeywell | 27
    Statuette | 32
    Circles | 34

QUADRANT II | 39
    Names | 41
    Lake of the Ozarks Parish | 44
    Theta Phi | 49
    Trifecta Resista | 53
    The Books | 57
    The Portrait | 60
    Higher Levels | 64
    Creation | 67
    Deception | 71

Song Liturgy | 75
The Barrel | 80
The Book of Books | 94
An Ant's Fantasy | 98

QUADRANT III | 103
An Open Window | 105
Garden | 109
Guns | 112
Mowing | 114
Waterfall | 116
The Sailboat | 119
Mac Computers | 122
Piles of Perplexities | 125
Healthy Religion | 132
On the Tillichian Road | 136

QUADRANT IV | 139
Out of the Nuclear Malaise | 141
Coveting Drones | 144
The Poor People's Campaign | 151
Real Significance | 156
The Value of Leisure | 160
Layers of Peacemaking | 166
Figment of Imagination | 170
Final Merging | 175

Appendix | 179
About the Author | 181
Books by the Author | 183

Preface

THIS MEMOIR OF A minister and peace activist in partnership with a whimsical ant celebrates a lifetime of artifacts in a Room that uncovers thinking about peace and justice issues, such as in the following themes:

- A "President of Chaos" jockeys for position with the Poor People's Campaign in an uncivil contest for values.
- The values of Jesus often give preference for insignificance—love for peace, too.
- A history of protests demonstrates against injustices and nuclear weapons.
- A backdrop of a ministerial career attempts to be prophetic in an unaware church.
- Disenfranchisement of democracy seems like wiping out a colony of ants and tagging them with tiny obituaries.
- Death ends up a normal part of nature and shows up in layers to enhance the cosmos.

This book is a valuable resource for thinking deeper about our whimsical insignificance and finding peace in the shadows.

Acknowledgements

To FELLOW RESISTERS OF Oppression and the great work of the Poor People's Campaign in 2018 and its continual support of Martin Luther King Jr., who recognized the evils of militarism, racism and poverty, also addressing in the Campaign environmental degradation.

To the best editor and peacemaker, Jane Stoever (truly indebted).

And other collaborators: Henry Stoever, Charles Carney, Jonne Long, Bob George, Bob Francis, Marcia Callis, Dale Shetler, including Ruthann Shetler and spa-peace-church friends.

To love K, Toni B. Faust, and her idea to use the stained-glass window as an illustration in the book and on the cover.

Quadrant I

InsignificANT

SOMETIMES I FEEL LIKE an ant.
Small and insignificant, mostly insignificant. I guess it is easy to feel small when some big bully comes along to step on you because that's what bullies do, but no, it's the insignificant thing that bothers you because you live in a cosmic world where everything matters and is far more important than you think.

And boom, something happens and the light switch is temporarily turned off. Complete darkness. The Room I live in shrinks to a few memories and I am just an ant ready to explore.

I crawled into this Room one day and started to climb the filing cabinet. It's located on one side of the room in what I call Quadrant I. In the corner is a beanbag with a red, white, blue and chartreuse quilt woven by my mother-in-law, Alice. On top of the beanbag are four pillows, very inviting, probably because they look soft and are excitingly colorful. This is where I spend most of my time, prostrate on the floor, deep in contemplation. Often in darkness.

Before figuring out how I climbed that cabinet, smooth and tall, I should introduce myself, a mere ant. My name is Ant X. I once thought about having others call me Mikie but that sounded like I would be stuck forever with poor self-esteem and sentimentality. Ant X provides a stronger name for an ego boost and the X part at the end of the name designates "X for the Spot" to mark the legs on the journey I'm about to take.

But I, the author, have been playing around with another possibility, that I am insignificANT like Ant X, if you don't mind the word pun. I once saw a cartoonish movie called ANT-Z that showed how the Workers and Warriors were divided into two caste systems and how the Warriors thought themselves superior. This book shows that insignificance is not so bad, that most of what we do adds up to a lot of insignificance. We spend much of our time trying to be something else and our antics wind up the same way—insignificant like Ant X. This is everyone's story and everyone's struggle to be different.

Is it really so odd that Ant X should go on this journey with me? Nobody is completely alone on a journey as long as one can talk to oneself. Sometimes it's confusing, which is which, the object of the conversation. That's a peculiar function of being a human being: having this ability to transcend oneself and carry on this conversation with a notion of God and what many call "prayer." But this companion is different, a mere ant named Ant X. Sometimes I am Ant X and sometimes I am me.

The amazing wonder is that Ant X represents a million ants for every human on the face of the earth, according to Wikipedia. Ants take up a third of the volume of living species, which means that there are lots of ants. When I woke up to the morning obituary and noticed a lot of deaths that barely had any comments, I wondered how many died insignificant deaths, probably alone and ignored. The morning news also reported a guy found in a truck at the airport, undiscovered for eight months. That's what this journey is about, facing the second evolution of life and the meaning of life when one is taken prematurely—just one of a million gone like a little ant without marking any spot.

Now Ant X is about to climb this filing cabinet—no small feat. Ant X is equipped with several features that make this black "honeypot" male especially good at scaling vertical walls. He could wedge himself between the opening of the filing doors. But he secretes a Pheromone from his back side and hind leg that puts pads on the surface of the wall and allows his feet to use hooks to grasp the surface. Pheromones also leave trails for other ants to follow and pick up the scent for foraging food. Ants have two elbow-like antennae that detect and communicate with their companions. Anyway the feat here is six small "feet" adaptable for climbing.

Now the filing cabinet that stores financial affairs is an uninteresting check and balance place to start this narrative. Actually there are two more cabinets but this happens to be the first one, creamy smooth and a holder of daily receipts, some of which are scattered on the top next to the phone before being bunched in the bottom files, one for entertainment, another folder for home improvement, and the last trifold for business and professional miscellany to be processed around tax time. It's just another part of the daily grind to be accountable—a pretense of one's insignificance.

Taxing

THE STORY BEGINS ON the precipice of the lower filing cabinet, which Ant X scales effortlessly. What happened was an audit and trial in 2010 over the years of 2005 and 2006, requiring volumes of paperwork and numerous lawyers and accountants. It was a story of resistance in a fright-and-fight world.

One can only conclude that those who use threats are trying to maintain control until they ratchet up the fear and turn to the use of force, invariably destructive. A dog-eat-dog world relies on the belief that the strong wins and that competing with others is the answer for survival of the fittest, which creates a selfish attitude more than a nurturing spirit. The tax code is meant to frighten and enforce people to stay in line, to submit to a slave mentality. More important, it is designed to keep the wealthy 1% in power and benefit a top-caste system. There is this feeling that the tax system benefits the military and the building of nuclear weapons, even though one has illusions of momentary benefits to the public when one receives a tax refund. Still, the tax system frightens and enforces compliance on a nation, which then can build patriotic zeal for sons and daughters to fight endless wars.

"I think we should have a dialogical moment," interrupted Ant X, perched precariously on the edge of this folder entitled "IRS Response."

I replied, "Are you afraid we will get into something that you will have to endure?"

"Well, yes," said Ant X, "like listening to a travelogue, often disgustingly boring because you cannot experience it yourself—only vicariously."

"Bear with me for a case study on the relevant parts," I retorted, "for everyone has a story to tell about the IRS."

"OK, I'll listen," said Ant X with his mandibles grinding, "but you have to realize that people get upset when they think that this attacks their patriotic duty."

Returning to the painful past is not a welcomed feeling. A slice of life trickled into my world like a slow-drip transfusion on February 25, 2008, announcing an audit that would last over four years and which still has its repercussions. When I met with the auditor a week later, I was sympathetic because I knew she was doing her job. However the audit cut open a bloody wedge that revealed two wounded perspectives.

During this time the auditor was targeting small businesses not making a profit, so she dismissed normally acceptable deductions like books and mileage. My business called MacLeisure Creations was an extension of many of the things I used to do in ministry like weddings and funerals and peace ministries. But it was primarily the writing of books, such as *GRAND PARENTING: Finding Roots and Wings for an Open Choice Generation*. My wife and I wrote this book together but it took a loss that first year even with our Family Life Playshops, sounding more fun than Workshops.

If I had made my deductions as a Minister instead of as a writer or small business owner, I might not have raised such red flags. It's difficult to say because I have not run across many auditors who understood the peculiar dynamics of ministry, particularly over the subject of being self-employed versus employed for social security purposes. Anyway, legitimate deductions made in the past were not being allowed.

This came at a crisis when I was trying to retire from some inner-city work. Years earlier, when I was starting the DREAM Center that stood for "Disciples Recreation Education And Ministry," I contracted with a YMCA, Neighborhood Association and

African American church as a means for youth to have an alternative to the streets. Always a lot was going on but I had some new stresses from the board over fundraising. The issue was the next step with the formidable IRS. I felt like an ant.

I wonder why I didn't give up. I scrambled around to various accountants and even hired a tax lawyer at great expense. I went to the manager but he felt obligated to back up his audit people. I requested to go to an appeals officer and started a lengthy journey of anxiously waiting for the next step.

Meanwhile I sought out some sympathetic cohorts among a group of tax resisters. I was always worried about association with such a group but I discovered some principled and courageous leaders who questioned the sizable bite that the military took from the budget—around 57%. It goes back and forth but the military gobbles up about 60%. I even sent some of these pamphlets through my correspondence since I no longer hid the fact that I felt that a large military budget subtracted from the needs of people and was on the wrong side of priorities between life and death. Of course the IRS saw this as frivolous and wasn't interested in moral arguments.

I sometimes wondered, "Am I dying?" It was a dark time, waiting or being provoked by the noise of an erratic fly or outside mower. Maybe this is it? A bunch of irritations always seem to scratch the surface of life's pleasantries. I was carrying heavy boxes around, which were volumes of transactions as well as emotional investment.

I realized that I had to do much of this alone. The lawyer had corporate background but was short on advice for specifics on ministry. I had to drop him after the initial huge fee but then he tried to double his fee. I was left with bulging shoeboxes of checks used for two questioned years and invoices spilling out of inflated vanilla folders. There was no turning back, just burdensome boxes to carry. It was an exercise in futility because each sorted category of checks was disputed as not professionally acceptable. Apparently there was a record-keeping system that was more correct. The question of one check denied the acceptance of all checks. It was futile. The passage of the audit was a lost cause. Having exhausted all appeals, I felt that the only recourse was to face tax court.

I never knew, not having been down this road before, if I would end up bankrupt. Losing our house was the main fear for my wife. Secondly, that she would have to visit me in prison. The penalties were mounting in interest every month. If you are poor you don't have a chance, and we were getting poorer. Our concerns heightened when the IRS changed strategies by sending letters to my wife. I always did the taxes so she was unfamiliar with some of the deduction strategies. But it seemed low to find new pressure points for collecting money but it also seemed like that was part of the game.

Maybe it was turning into a game. The IRS was out to collect money for national defense, and those who raised questions about killing others in war resisted as conscientious objectors. Militarism infiltrates every facet of our lives and the USA does half the world's military spending. A trillion here and there pile up the national debt but we have the illusion that it stimulates the economy. It probably does for contractors and corporations that continue to make weapons that we don't need. That's one place we won't find an audit and accountability like we force on individuals to pay for what we don't need. The game is complicated.

I actually tried to learn strategies. In the 1990s, I worked for a season with IRS for no other reason than to be unafraid of them. It was a secretive place; you entered the place with badges and codes. Once we were threatened with Anthrax detected on the seal of an envelope The bacteria from cattle could affect skin and lungs. We were quarantined and doused with chemicals. Fear causes an overreaction in which officials go to great lengths to protect others, sometimes too late and too exaggerated. It's difficult for the IRS to trust the public much of the time, so this adversarial relationship is spawned.

They started sending certified letters to my mate. They were taking money from the Social Security check of my wife. The action was increasing. Penalties were increasing even before the court date. A three-hour meeting was set up to dispute piles of receipts and checks rather than philosophical questions about self-employment status, housing allowance and other issues related to the case. It was a nightmare setting up the court date that often shifted. Like I said, it's complicated.

I just never had enough information to satisfy the government. They were trying to wear me down by micromanaging the receipts and calling for a business plan. The point seemed to be that you could never have enough documents. It was like talking in a foreign language to those who could not interpret the wider understanding of Church, the difference between local church and universal Church. I was becoming more convinced that this might be a peacemaking moment. Dauntingly, I was nearing over two years of obstacles toward the court time on May 26, 2010.

I stood on the shiny third floor of the Federal Court Building and stared out over the mall before the City Hall of Kansas City. I was in awe. I knew this was big. I was a mere Ant. I reverently went into the courtroom with my friend-lawyer Convener of PeaceWorks, who was disqualified from representing me since he was not registered with the tax court. But he was there, silently in moral support. I was resolved to face what I must face.

The tall, neatly dressed, fresh-out-of-law-school prosecutor stood before the non-frivolous judge and presented the case, to the best of the law, that all deductions Schedule C and A were rejected. Quickly, my opening statement followed. "Your Honor, the IRS auditor pointed out that my small business, MacLeisure Creations, did not show enough profit and dismissed my deductions in Schedule C without considering legitimate deductions that I would make as a self-employed minister. I will show that my tax filing was made in good faith and should include legitimate deductions."

I introduced myself by defining the groups I belong to such as Interfaith Worker Justice for economic justice, Reclaim Democracy for the Walmart campaign, American Friends Service Committee for raising a conscience about immoral wars, Disciples Peace Fellowship for a conscience of peace in the Church, Peace Works for stopping nuclear weapons, and Interfaith Justice Advocacy of Immigrants for supporting immigrants against deportation.

"Oomph, may I break in here?" interrupted Ant X.

"Well, you're just like the prosecutor," I exclaimed. "When she heard me go through this three-and-a-half hour testimony on each of the allowable deductions especially the half off for Entertainment expenses, I made the flippant comment, 'That's the way the rich do it.'"

Ant X gestured with his outstretched antennae swinging wildly, "What did she say?"

I responded, "She shouted out, 'Irrelevant. Immaterial.' So I withdrew the comment, but I had made my point."

"Did you really do this for three-and-a-half hours?" inquired Ant X, striking his right antenna across his head.

"I was exhausted by this time," I replied. "I was ready for a closing statement after the prosecutor closed her case."

Ant X was impatient, ready to move on.

I recall some of what I said that day: "Your Honor, upon hearing the evidence I can only agree to disagree. I have reason to believe that my deductions were legitimate. My business plan shows my intent at making a profit, but, since this is not a salient point, I want to emphasize that MacLeisure Creations is an extension of my role as a self-employed minister, which means that I can take deductions related to my housing allowance and auto expenses. The deductions are ordinary and necessary to my work as a minister and motivated by certain higher values that don't always fit in a profit-driven system as documented in my book *GAPS* in the search for peace, justice, creation, openness, love and authenticity.

"Also I am here trying to understand this complicated tax impasse because I don't have the answers but the answer for me is not to support war and its weapons." I pulled out and unfolded a pamphlet that showed the 57% red graph of the military spending for defense, war, and nuclear weapons programs and the diminutive amounts to other departments like education. On the other side is the title, "One Minute for Peace" and a quote from Dwight D. Eisenhower: "Every gun that is made, every warship launched, every rocket fired, signifies in the final sense a theft from those who hunger and are not fed, those who are cold and not clothed."

I continued, "Perhaps we can't fix the system but that doesn't mean we shouldn't try to seek a moral centeredness free from weapons and an integrity with our tax codes. I have submitted my side. I thank you for hearing my case."

I guess I thought the Judge would render his verdict immediately but he said that it would come in August and he muttered something about my concluding comments and that he would have to take another look at the penalties. Nevertheless I felt that the Judge listened and was sympathetic to the case.

Actually these things never seem to finish. I never heard from the Judge in August, never heard from anyone for a year and a half, and then a suspiciously terse letter came from the prosecutor, not from the Judge, that we were levied taxes and it would come out of Social Security. It just seemed to happen arbitrarily with monthly withdrawals but it was never by our consent or agreement with any verdict or hearsay from a prosecutor who needed to win in a start-up career. All seemed ambiguous and sneaky and trivial. Frankly I felt the IRS was stealing money that was not theirs for some two years, but that was their problem. We had let it go by then and relished the afterglow of the "event."

Ant X, overhearing all this, asked, "What do you mean? Event?"

"For two days I was beaming inside and marveling at my capacity to face the music, because I have always been basically shy and felt uneasy about any presentation before others." I smiled. "I kept saying to myself that I can not believe I did that!"

"Did you feel like it was worth all the time you spent preparing to go to court?" Ant X asked.

"I don't know if we felt like we had a choice, but I do feel like it was an event, something special that tested our character." I remember wistfully staring from the high tier of the magnificent stage of the Federal Courthouse. "I guess I would do it again to duplicate that feeling."

Taxing

"I suspect you will," said Ant X. "But how can you say what you did was significant when you don't know if you won or lost?"

"But you see, uncertain results, but I won!"

Jobs

SCATTERED OVER THE TOP of the cabinet is a small pile of receipts ready to be squeezed between folders. This method replaced weekly accounting of expense sheets and saved time throughout the year until the burden of tax time around April 15. The advent of computers offered an answer for filling out income taxes and made it possible to create neat copies.

The idea of becoming a war resister was frightening. Most of the time, resisters try to avoid audit events like the above narrative. Most war resisters keep their incomes under the radar. Some find ways to maintain home businesses or high deductions. Others boldly indicate that they are withholding half their tax income because of military spending, directing the monies to more constructive causes and facing the consequences when Uncle Sam calls them to "ante" up. There is a high cost in having principles, particularly the criticism that comes from challenging the tax system.

"Interesting that the word 'ant' may have a distant relationship to 'ante,' meaning 'pay up to gamble' or 'before.' I have a hunch that you—a mere Ant—were here long before humans and we could probably bet that you will be here long after," I enviously noted.

"Maybe. I only take one step at a time," Ant X observed. "What's next?"

"Shall we climb upward?"

Ant X had no problem moving out of the lower drawer but faced more difficulty climbing the second drawer. He could move easier on top of the cabinet but had to negotiate a jump to the other tall and grey filing cabinet displaying a slew of magnetized business cards. Most of them were contacts for home improvement but one of them stood out. The rainbow colored letters prominently said, "Support Greenpeace." Ant X perched himself on top of a miniature pickle wearing a superhero cape with the letters SP (Super Pickle).

"Ant X, there is a story here worth sharing." I stroked my beard, reminiscing.

Greenpeace is an environmental group that used to maintain an office in Kansas City. Internationally known for sailing the Rainbow Warrior and harassing whaling vessels, Greenpeace aggressively confronted ecology abusers. The local office would gather canvassers each day, orient them to activities around the world and assign them to blocks in the city. A couple of vans would drop individuals or couples off in various areas and pick them up late at night.

The local office had excellent managers who were efficient in handling money, nurturing to young people and patient with older adults. It was a challenge to keep up with the latest ecology concern and how to improve the presentation to go door-to-door. I was one of the older ones.

"I was looking for the perfect job," I explained to Ant X. "I decided that ministry had some advantages in providing thinking time but it had some limitations on how much you could say honestly. It depended on the progressive vision of the congregation, but mostly they were locked into nationalism and control. The congregations I served were autonomous and lay governed. I remember thinking that people were drawn to church for its ideals and turned pragmatic and over-protective of the building. I will never forget an Elder who came up to me back in the days of Vietnam when I shared a sermon on the pride of nations and the need to admit when we were wrong. The Elder threatened me, 'If you ever preach a sermon like that again, you're out of here.'

"Guess what? I of course gave a similar sermon and lost my ministry," I told Ant X, somewhat gratified by the events that spoke truth to power.

Soon I was searching for something different. I found it in Greenpeace. I enjoyed the young people and felt like a mentor for some, I liked the conversations with some of the neighbors, and I thought I was doing something important, out to save the world. However I remember how scared people were. Sometimes I met disturbed people with shotguns. The wealthier homes were fortresses of fear. It was risky and a difficult way to make a living. I was still looking for the perfect job.

"This is a higher climb," said Ant X, trying to grasp the smooth side.

"It ought to be an escalation in higher education," I said. "This cabinet contains a bank of knowledge from the lower level of undergraduate training to higher levels of seminars and critical thinking. I'm not even sure that college is enough to enable people to discern political thinking because technical knowledge might run a computer but graduates may fail to understand moral values. It takes the humanities and experience to shape compassionate students who will start to dismantle institutional injustices."

Ant X was struggling to climb. He advised, "It would be so much easier to say, 'OK, Google,' ask the question, get the answer, than go through the rigor of these courses."

"The point is," I explained, "an education is so much more than coming up with the correct answer as if you were playing TV's 'Jeopardy.' Life is full of ambiguity, and sometimes you have to discern the better choice when both choices make sense. Sometimes we have to hold contradictions as both valid for our lives.

"Much of the time education is unlearning," I continued, "unlearning what we thought we knew, making room for better ideas."

"What good is that?" pondered Ant X. "Just a waste of time."

"Possibly!" I nodded in agreement. "I wanted to stop and lift up some of the courses. I wanted to check the syllabuses and pore through the tests and see my grades. You know what?"

"What are you saying?" asked Ant X with a quizzical look.

"Ecclesiastes!"
"What?"
"Vanity. Vanity. All is vanity."
"What?"
"I don't care anymore," I surprisingly said. "These files are packed with essays and class notes; I have no desire to reread them."
"What does that mean?" inquired Ant X.
"What was once significant has moved into the realm of insignificance," I observed with befuddlement, knowing that if I departed from all these papers, only a small part would remain inside me.
"Time to move on," challenged Ant X.
"One step at a time," I said. "Life is transient, constantly changing what is significant."

During a period of time in my 50s, I was trying to find the perfect job. I would check the job listings to discover plenty of low-wage jobs and in many cases I was over-qualified with irrelevant credentials. No matter what, jobs are not that easy to find.

I did enjoy the creativity of becoming the Coordinator for the DREAM Center. University Heights Christian Church closed on Forest and 56th Street on the Missouri side and my job description was to do inner-city work with a facility that had a gym. I contracted with the YMCA to make their programs available, provided office space for the 49-63 Neighborhood Association and made arrangements with an African American congregation. The DREAM Center stood for "Disciples Recreation Education And Ministry." Programs provided an alternative to the streets but the maintenance costs were high. It was a good program and met needs for people struggling to survive. After about ten years it ran its course and the monies disappeared. It was a challenging job while it lasted, but never the perfect job in which one has control of one's destiny, as is the case with writing. I concluded that significance takes a lifetime and for me I had to wait for retirement to find the perfect job.

Games

Ant X hiked his path to the top. "Hooray, I made it."
He looked around. "This looks like a chessboard."

Carved onyx chessmen stood on the shiny, marble-like, dual matching squares of the chessboard. The beautiful set, acquired in a once-in-a-lifetime trip to Acapulco, reminds one of both travel and challenge. When you have a grandson who likes to play chess, you are gratified to give him the tools to think two or three moves ahead. In other words, one can learn to think in terms of consequences. One can learn discipline to restrain impulsive and ignorant behavior. Chess is a good teacher about life and sportsmanship.

Chess, perceived as a game for intelligent people, offers a high level of competition. When one competes for grades or plays sports, one rivals another for the top prize. Then competition becomes a problem in promoting aggressive behavior, to outwit, to outdo one's opponent. The American way is to value winners over losers.

Taking time out to analyze competition, one notices a hierarchy of social values, where men are valued over women, or whites over blacks, or rich over poor. Whenever one is valued over the other, that dehumanizes the other group. White rich men who belong to a white privileged class discriminate against others. They are racists, not necessarily on a personal level but on a public level, because they belong to a racist society. In this certain sense, we are all racists, black and white, because we participate in a society that discriminates. We are unequal. Thus we set up a caste system that makes some better than others and makes some feel insignificant.

Ant X observed, "Is that a problem for humans?"

I replied with some passion, "The sooner one recognizes that competition causes a lot of tension, the better. One can still allow some competition in sports but not to have to be a winner all the time. A great burden is lifted when one no longer has to compete to be superior to another. Racism is removed. Relationships improve. Name-calling is unnecessary. Flow of living is easier. Health is enhanced. One no longer has to prove that one is better than another. One starts to get along with other people, with fewer stereotypes and less fear."

"Maybe you can get along with an ant," giggled Ant X, wiggling.

"As long as you're not a pest when there are too many of you," I countered.

The next day I plopped myself into the beanbag, snuggled into the puffy blanket and quickly closed my eyes. Darkness pulled me into a comfortable world, into a safe room. Of course it's also a confessional world in which I have to admit that sadness overtakes me every time I think how a President of Chaos could be elected. Every core value that I hold dear is under attack as if a two-year-old wandered through a Trump romper room and gleefully pushed over all the blocks.

My Room is full of darkness every time I think how many were duped into following President Chaos. I wonder if his charm represents the opposite of what you would think, how low you can go, how crude you can be and still get away with it. In house upon household, families honor the rule that we do not talk politics or religion under this roof. Meaningful discussion is muted to avoid divided households. Trivial concerns move in. People are limited in discerning political differences. Many are consigned to a world of insignificance or reduced to amusing themselves through TV, another way to experience the trivial wasteland. The feeling of darkness lasts a long time, but not forever.

"What's this?" noticed Ant X.

The other game on top of the chessboard was a cribbage board, ready to be picked up by a grandchild. What a great game—dealing out cards to move pegs to be the first to reach 120 holes. In cribbage, considered one of the best two-handed games, a player discards two cards to the dealer's crib and cuts the deck to count points from five cards. What is fascinating about the game is the variety of three- or four-handed runs and the multiple ways to find fifteen 2s. If you can add to fifteen, you will have fun with this game. The highest total of this game is a hand of twenty-nine, by holding three 5s and a jack of the suit of the 5 that is cut from the deck.

The thread that runs through this game is camaraderie of playfulness that is passed from generation to generation. It's a relaxing game for two people that pulls one out of darkness into a friendly, enjoyable activity. Cribbage moves you outside of your loneliness. I don't know why I've only seen men play the game, perhaps because I was one of the participants stuck in a room with another, but of course computers now can change the players. Technology alters the game and surpasses the limits of humans as evidenced in the ability of computers to outsmart even master chess players. Even though a computer could play cribbage, it still maintains that charm by holding onto a thread of our humanity, simple to play and fun to do.

Some things seem not to change. Rarely has a piece moved. I can lie hours in the beanbag chair and sense that the world is dependable, albeit that is an illusion about stability. But games give a restorative faith that life can go forward.

Peace

ONE OF THE ANCHORS of life is a belief in peace, reaffirmed in a Living Witness Award mounted high on the First Quadrant wall. I call out to Ant X, "Go up to that plaque and remind me what it says."

Even though I have heard it before, I love the melody of the words:

> The members and friends of Disciples Peace Fellowship of Greater Kansas City are proud and glad to make the presentation of the "Living Witness Award" to a person who has exemplified the virtues of peacemaking throughout a long and famous journey of witnessing to the validity and power of Christian love. Throughout both vocational and avocational pursuits, there has been ample evidence garnered from the exemplary witness for this high tribute . . .
>
> —an abiding commitment to peace and justice, locally and globally
>
> —a persistence in advocating peace and justice for others
>
> —a peacefulness with self and toward others
>
> —a faith maturity which serves as a model for all who would walk the Christian path
>
> —a pastor's heart which burns with a prophet of fire.
>
> For such achievements and characteristics and so much more, we honor
>
> Ronald L. Faust
>
> October 9, 2003

Disciples Peace Fellowship

The award carries the usual signatures, except that AC Cuppy was unusually committed to peace actions. I guess he'll try to live to be a hundred, and may make it. He did. He was someone I admired for missionary work in the Congo and Habitat for Humanity involvement. He was a Disciples Minister along with his wife, VG, who set a high standard for peacemaking. I guess if I were to add another characteristic to the above honor it would be the willingness to take some risks against the injustices of war because a lot of ministers play it safe rather than lose their jobs. AC did not play it safe. The names of both AC and VG Cuppy were on a special plaque that hung in the Regional Office for many years.

The recognition that the Disciples Peace Fellowship gave me was significant and arbitrary. No one person does peacemaking alone. The individual may have the yearning but it takes a community for one to be a peacemaker. Within the community every one may be a peacemaker but to engage in bold action requires the support of the community, because risky action often means jail and court time. The state has a different notion of what it means to be patriotic.

Defiantly crossing his antennae, Ant X decided to enter the fray about how difficult it is to find peace: "I mean, I don't get it. All we discover is constant war. Why is that?"

"I wonder if part of the answer is the way we view patriotism. War would come easy if our attitude is 'Love it or leave it!'"

"That's about what we have in a country full of hate and exclusion of immigrants!" Ant X acknowledged.

"It's worse than that," I offered. "Patriotism blocks peace when we use the motto, 'America, love it and salute it.'"

"What do you mean by that?" Ant X was intrigued.

"It's what some might call 'civil religion,' honoring the state above religion, making militarism far more important than anything else."

I continued, "A false patriotism honors the country with national songs, service costumes, pledge of allegiance, standing at attention and removing hats to show respect for the use of force." I bowed down despondently for all the wrong reasons.

The ant shuttered.

So I took a different tack. "You know, 'I told him,' another kind of patriotism follows the motto, 'Love it and improve it!' True patriots can handle constructive criticism, build community involvement, resolve issues, reduce noise and exhibit kindness."

Ant X replied, "You're talking about the improvement of the country, not just singing about it and allowing the wrongs to pass us by."

"That's right. Not a shallow, dressed-up patriotism of noise and empty promises," I vowed, "but a genuine love of our country, working for peace and justice."

When the Nobel Peace Prize was awarded to the International Campaign to Abolish Nuclear Weapons (ICAN) in 2017, it lent support to the entire peace community. This award recognized 122 nations that banned nuclear weapons as against the few nations that possessed them. The nuclear nations had been holding the rest of the nations hostage to their control, but no longer.

"Remember when groups would claim certain areas to be Shalom Zones and not everybody would join?" I asked Ant X. "You could designate a part as a peace zone and still carry the message for peace."

"It looks like the Peace Prize will go a long way to tell those that want to keep their weapons that they may be on a suicidal path without benefits," suggested Ant X, jumping around with excitement.

The peace community tries to communicate its message at great odds, such as the Disciples Peace Fellowship in its calls for peace during times of war. The DPF has an illustrious history as the oldest peace group of a mainline denomination. In 1935, 75 people concerned about peace met at the Convention of the Christian Church (Disciples of Christ) in San Antonio, Texas, to form the DPF. Central to the church's heritage and promoted by founder Alexander Campbell, DPF has been keeping alive the passion for peace and justice. Disciples Peace Fellowship is an independent organization affiliated with the Christian Church (Disciples of Christ). Since 1935, the DPF has served as a leaven within our denomination and in the larger community, pressing for action toward the elimination of war, giving support to conscientious objectors, mentoring Peace Interns and fostering the use of nonviolence in relationships. The original covenant of DPF includes working to abolish war and to create the conditions of peace and justice among all people and nations. The DPF recognizes that to work for peace, we must work for justice. That work centers on both education and action.

"*Blessed are the peacemakers, for they shall be called children of God.*"—Matthew 5:9

The founding meeting for DPFKC started on Peace Sunday with a Peace Feast on December 7, 1986, in Community Christian Church. Following meaningful worship with Garnet Day, DPF national Executive Secretary, and David Downing, national President of DPF for 1987, thirty persons submitted applications and dues to become members of the Kansas City DPF chapter.

During this time newsletters came out such as the "Voice of the Turtle," taking its name from Song of Solomon 2:12—"*The flowers appear on the earth, the time of singing has come, and the voice of the turtle is heard in our land*" (KJV). Some of the first quotes in this quarterly newsletter were as follows:

"*Speak, move, act in peace, as if you were in prayer. In truth, this is prayer.*"—Francis de S. Fenelon

"*A peace is of the nature of a conquest; for then both parties nobly are subdued, and neither party loser.*"—William Shakespeare

In 1993 I became a convener for the group. My goal was to make a conscientious effort in the Regional Church to make peace a priority of the prophetic function of the church. We were an active group until 2016 even though we continue with a Website dpfkc.faithweb.com and feature a plaque of peacemakers at one of our peace churches, New Song Christian Church. Most of the peacemaking activity continues to support PeaceWorksKC.org.

National Security Campus (nuclear weapon complex)

Honeywell

IN 2010 FOUR OF us blocked the entrance to the Honeywell Plant in Kansas City. This was the first time that anyone had raised questions about why illnesses were showing up among workers. Managed by companies such as Bendix, Allied Signal and Honeywell, the Kansas City Plant produced non-nuclear parts for nuclear weapons; it manufactured the fuses, the radar equipment and the nuclear triggers that made the weapons work. But most employees were told that it was non-nuclear, free of radioactivity, and that the nuclear components of the end products, nuclear weapons, were the plutonium stored in Los Alamos, New Mexico, or the uranium in Oak Ridge, Tennessee.

Almost nobody had any idea what was going on in this national security center, before it was even called something similar. Apparently that is what the government wanted in order to keep secret anything that might alarm the public, like the spread of radioactivity. People were singing the praises of a good job, with good benefits and good wages. People would go to work, pass checkpoints, not raise questions and at the end of the day go home to their families. It was a good life until these cancers and lung diseases showed up.

Ant X was exploring the top of the filing cabinet and felt the need to break into the silence. "So all workers are quiet like me?"

"It is believed that the less you know about the inner workings of the plant, the better off you will be," I noted. "Silence is golden, just do your job!"

Ant X thought about this for the longest time. "If something happens to you later on, and you don't know anything, then it will be hard to link any products to what was happening to you."

"I think you see a pattern here," I said, in one of those aha moments.

Ant X chimed in, "Keep everything quiet. Never be accountable. Blame other things for any troubles."

This plant was an integral part of the Cold War, joining the code of silence. In the '60s the work force jumped from 3,000 to 9,000, producing a stockpile of parts for the barrage of weapons that would scare nations from launching them before going MAD, i.e., into "Mutually Assured Destruction." Workers were exposed to all kinds of toxic material without their knowledge.

When numbers started coming forth concerning an unusual amount of cancers, with families reporting that some 154 workers had died from toxins at the Kansas City Plant, an investigation commenced. One of the participants who emerged from the silence was Maurice Copeland, who rose to a position of supervisor and finally saw too much to continue, after working at the plant for 32 years. He is a whistleblower who has sounded the alarm on the cover-up of chemical materials. What was supposed to be non-nuclear was sometimes radioactive, and the federal government documented radioactive spills at the plant. One of the activists who made a great contribution in understanding the chemical and nuclear connections was a nurse, Ann Suellentrop, who represented Physicians for Social Responsibility and informed us of the dangers of radioactivity.

Over 2000 hazardous chemicals were detected on Bannister Federal Complex, home to the Kansas City Plant, which from 1949 to 2014 made parts for nuclear weapons. Some of those chemicals were radioactive. A heavy dose of beryllium was found at the complex, reduced to 2% concentration to make it acceptable for human adaptability. Deadly either way, eventually. But many workers are denied claims since families are unable to prove any link of the illnesses to the plant. Suspicion without documentation is not enough to be conclusive for the government. Dangerous toxins were treated casually around unprotected workers, who appeared to be casualties sacrificed for national defense.

What I remember about working for the IRS, back in the '90s, was the secrecy. I went to work, did my job and came home knowing that I would receive a paycheck. I had no idea what they did next door at the Kansas City Plant, also part of the Bannister Federal Complex. That's the way it was. Questions were kept to yourself. Public awareness on what happened in these federal facilities was muted, until one day in 2010 protesters showed up—almost 61 years after the plant began its nuclear weapons work.

Peacemakers gathered at the entrance way and after several statements and a poem, four of us did not move when ordered to do so. Two Catholic Workers, Frank Cordaro from Des Moines and Steven Jacobs from Columbia, and two PeaceWorks members from the Kansas City area, Jane Stoever and I, blocked the gate on July 18, 2010, reading poetry and not heeding orders from security police. We were handcuffed, placed in vehicles and driven to a nearby detention area where we were processed and issued tickets for court appearances. Three of us paid fines but Jane Stoever elected to appear in court on August 6 that year.

At the time we did not realize the full implication of this protest. Jane made a beautiful statement in court and accepted the punishment of community service, which she did with her usual duties at the Holy Family Catholic Worker House. She showed the rest of us that if we wished to follow this pattern of civil disobedience, we could speak out in court in this way and use the media to draw attention to the buildup of the nuclear weapons arsenal and its dangers. Stories of cancer, the subterfuge of wasteful spending and the toxic threats to society emerged from the protests. This beginning protest laid the groundwork for a citywide public vote on preventing further spending on a new nuclear weapons plant and many hearings, although the pushback on the ethical issues was lost in the noise for jobs. But still the issue was more in the open on what was happening at the new National Security Campus.

Ant X was poised high on top of the Living Witness Award, pondering. "One can look back at that event, wondering if it made a difference?"

"I know . . . I know . . . it took a lot of time and worry," I said.

Ant X noted, "I bet a lot of details have faded into the past."

"They have, but the significance of what we did remains strong." I nostalgically paused. "Remembering the eyes of the others and looking deep into the soul of their robust spirit, we bonded."

Ant X contemplated the moment. "So I have been told that there have been over 100 instances of a person being arrested and checked through the courts in subsequent trials, but it started with the Feisty Four."

Thus it began. PeaceWorks was a big part of it. Jane Stoever was the first to witness in court. Henry Stoever was our lawyer who later argued and won his own case for civil disobedience. Brave persons came forth to stand on principle and for peace.

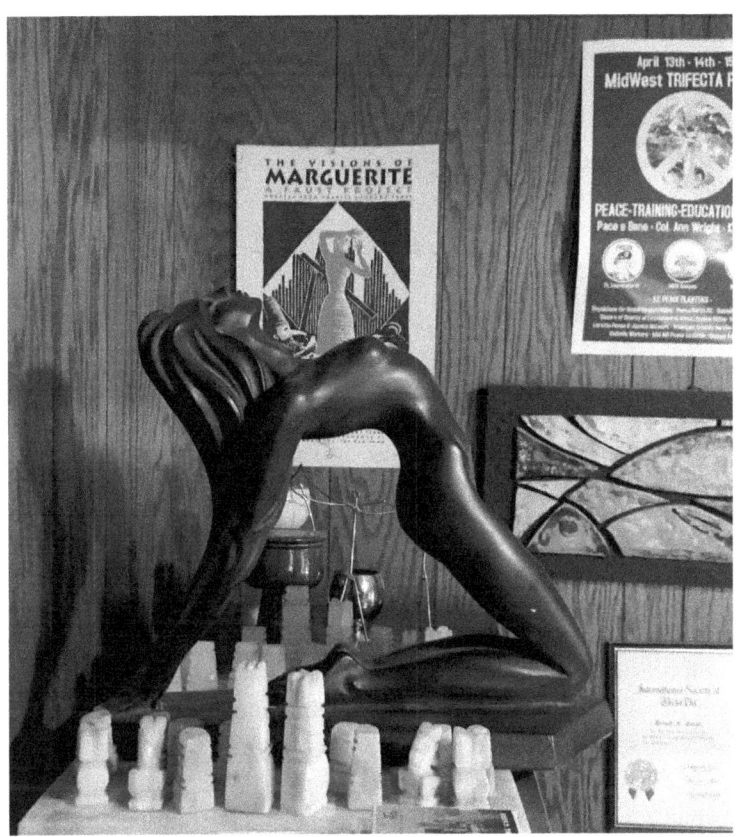

Statuette

Statuette

Peering up at the next icon of the Room, I dreamily declared, "It was a good memory."

What emerged was a statue of Beauty, dark, curvaceous, exuding sexuality. She held a prominent place on top of the filing cabinet as Queen of Attraction.

This statue to femininity demonstrates a woman kneeling in a back bend, propped up by her outstretched arms reaching backward and supported on a pedestal with her finely chiseled face and soft breast jutted upward while her long hair is draped downward on her arms and flows dramatically in penetrable waves. She always deserves a second glance.

This is art permanently and personally inspired in a time when the search for love quickly disappears in transient amnesia. The search is life-long; the experience of sex is temporary. Efforts to win over mortality are futile. We are actually earthy nerds, trying to be boastfully cool, when what we really need is to be excruciatingly honest, admitting our vulnerability, admitting our femininity.

"It's all so vain," said tiny Ant X, stretching to see the top.

"It is nice to look up to this statue once in a while," I uttered in profound disgust, "because it might be our last time."

Ant X added to this discussion, "Statues like this give us the illusion of permanence."

"And omniscience." I lit up, "The reminders of sex, its receptivity and its desire to connect, are so profoundly woven into the receptors of our brains, that it is difficult to ignore with all these visuals except to control it."

"Well, the search is on," Ant X panted, coming off the pedestal of this strikingly beautiful statuette. "I am going to find my honey Queen someday, maybe on this trip."

"Is the ant world so much different from the human fantasy for sex," I asked, "except smaller? Now, how does this ultimate honeymoon flight go in the ant world?"

Ant X answered, "During the Nuptial flight the male ants (Drones) and the to-be Queen fly to mate. She teases the males by flying faster to determine the more capable or competent among them. Other reports have the drones leading out and leaving a pheromone path to follow. Copulation can mean that the end is near."

"What are you talking about?" I eagerly asked.

"Well, it's pretty elementary," Ant X interjected. "In ant society male ants serve one purpose: inseminate the queen."

"Life down to the basics, I guess," I added.

Ant X shared more. "Unfortunately, as legend goes, the male's stomach can literally explode from too much sex, which causes his death, and the Queen, losing her wings, goes on to lay an overpopulated abundance of eggs. There are variations of this story, but you get the point. The male will fly anywhere to fulfill his destiny and die happily ever after."

Circles

THE JOURNEY WAS ABOUT to enter into a trail of Circles. First on the trail were these large candles big enough across that the wick would burn in the center without spilling wax over the side. Always impressive, such candles were highlights for worship, focusing attention on the flickering light. Holding a smaller upright candle, a nightstand stood apart for its embossed turquoise and gold sides. The candle reminded me of something that Dr. Scrooge might carry from room to room looking for ghosts, or signs from the mystical sphere.

One of the more playful circles was an art piece that showed caricatures of dancers holding arms and silver legs in a display of exuberance. Obviously celebrative, the dance encircled a container that looked like a candle but consisted of gray, dark, smooth rocks. These were the kind of rocks that could twirl in a pocket and become pet smoothies.

Then Ant X arrived at a collection of chalices. Two of the cups were distinctive for their shiny gold finish; another was a bronze clay-shaped cup with a lid on top. The fourth chalice stood taller than the others and featured a cream-colored large stem. The maze of chalices was significant for their connection with a cup of the Christian Church (Disciples of Christ), which has a logo of a red chalice with a St. Andrew's cross on its side, representing Scottish Presbyterian roots. The logo was elegantly uncomplicated in its meaning by pointing to the centrality of the Lord's Supper when people gathered to be Church. The Disciples are noted for engaging in Communion every Sunday and many ecumenical efforts to cooperate with other churches around the Table.

"I made a career as a Disciples Minister because I liked the democratic feel of the denomination, but sometimes democracy doesn't always work out," I exclaimed, "Look what happened to the 2016 political election when we put someone destructive in positions of authority."

"I would think democracy would be desirable," Ant X interjected.

"It is, but it doesn't treat the power of evil seriously enough," I retorted. "Autocratic arm-twisting, law-and-order tactics, and militaristic attitudes tend to take over and destroy community. Hierarchal structures hold the bullies in check and make it easier to do social justice."

"Do you really think a chalice could stop a bully?" Ant X crossed his antennae in disbelief.

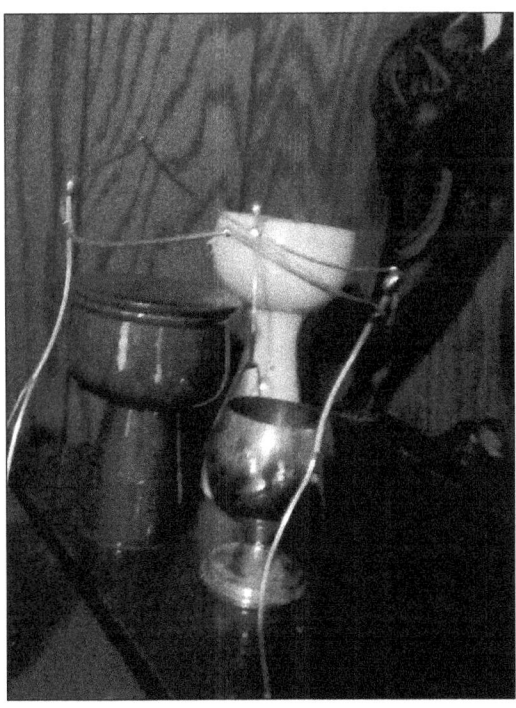

I felt preachy. "The intent is so pure when it sends the message that all are welcome around the Table, that no matter how awful we are, we are included, we are equal, we are poor in spirit, we are accepted. And those who want to carry the guns and justify war . . . "

"Maybe they can catch up before they do too much damage," said Ant X hopefully, tipping his right antenna to the ceiling.

"That's what we are talking about! Which side will hold the balance? Constructive or destructive. Building up or tearing down. Generosity or greed. Life or death." I added, "It's all about change."

"What difference does it make what we do on this planet?" asked the inquisitive Ant X.

I paused before answering, "Maybe it accumulates the energy one way or the other, whereby we amass value points of goodness or we create black holes of nothingness."

"Will that drive us into oblivion or into a more exciting future?" Ant X pondered.

"Yet to be determined," I said. "I saw the reports of Astrophysicists that claim that they spotted a collision of two black holes on August 17, 2017, that created a 'kilonova.' They recorded a picture that looks like my painting by Leonardo Niermann that offers both a flash of light of geometric colors and the ripple effect of a gravitational pull. That's what excites the scientists. They can now detect gravitational waves, traveling at light speed, sucking matter into black holes."

"I don't understand it. I'm only an ant," stuttered Ant X.

"We can only grasp so much," I noted, "but it seems to me that it would make sense to keep the human enterprise going forward rather than blowing it up with our nuclear weapons."

I slumped into the beanbag chair and a weighty gravitational blanket covered my face in darkness. My thoughts turned down dead end roads. I was saddened when I wondered how people in a democracy could elect a President who was tailspinning a nation into "ruination," systematically taking apart a nation just for his amusement. I could be thinking this and it could all end, unless some gravitational pull intervenes to pull back the President's finger off the nuclear button. The Room was full of darkness.

Circles

I looked up and saw a fleet of miniature sailboats on top of the cabinet. One of the boats was a lampstand looking blue and nautical with cloth masts. There was Ant X sitting in this make-believe sailboat, thoroughly relaxed. It reminded me of another sailboat event.

My friend and I were relaxed in my sailboat, Sabbatical II, when the flight of the Eagle, Hawk and Blue Heron took place. I watched the free-fall dive of the Hawk pell-mell out of the sky, over the mast into the water. It thrust itself headlong into a huge splash, twisted itself, and then thrust itself from the surface of the lake and flew east toward the trees with a white flash of fish in its talons. Later, a flurry of dramatic movement covered the sky with the white flutter of wings of the Eagle chasing the Hawk, causing the prey of huge fish to fall into the water while the Blue Heron escaped with his life from both hunters. The Eagle returned to his high perch on the barren tree, alone and foiled in his thievery.

Ant X observed, "You tell a nice story of survival of the fittest in the bigger circle of life. What's that supposed to mean in the total significance of things?"

"That's what we are exploring in this book," I said, as my eyes were turning to the next wall.

"There is too much here," chimed in Ant X. "Every time you stop, suddenly it becomes significant."

Beanbag

Quadrant II

Names

WHAT'S IN A NAME? When you walk toward Quadrant II the way Ant X the Ant does, you confront a huge poster entitled, "The Visions of Marguerite: A Faust Project." The Faust name is a bold statement of historic significance, outlining a universal theme of selling one's soul to eternal darkness in exchange for all the pleasures of the world. This popular opera in the late 1800s follows the trials of Faust, a philosopher and metaphysical professor who no longer receives satisfaction from his studies. In fact he feels he missed out on much of life and love because of his academic pursuits and wants to experience a different direction, which leads him to make a compact with Mephistopheles, a congenial friend of the Underworld. Faust eventually seduces a young maiden, Marguerite, who bears their child but is put in prison over the child's death. Faust has one of the visions that images and puts him in voice contact with Marguerite, where he serenades his love but her brother resents this relationship. A fight ensues, the brother dies, not before he assigns Marguerite to a tragic end. But then she has a vision.

    Marguerite rises into heaven, surrounded by a chorus that sings,

> "Christ hath risen!
> Peace and felicity
> To all disciples of the Master!
> Christ hath arisen!"

Falling to his knees, Faust experiences shock and awe. Supernatural forces ban Mephistopheles from interfering. Having a two-tier universe divided into Heaven and Hell makes it easier to imagine that we find our significance rising toward Heaven. The opera ends like we might image death, alone and without intense romance but with a chorale singing about Heaven.

What's in a name? Identity. Significance. Connection. Many who feel insignificant write their name into a permanent ledger. Much of the motivation for leaving large sums of money to institutions is to put a name on a plaque or a room or a street or any place that says you were important. By contrast, many mass murderers do diabolical deeds with devastating consequences because they want to be remembered for the sheer excitement of the event. The twisted logic of the event identifies their place in history, not their contribution.

"Crossing the stage to receive my High School diploma was the most embarrassing moment of my life, so I thought, because it meant that I just changed my name," I told Ant X. "Suddenly I was no one. Nobody would remember that I was a top ten scholar, that I had some success as a wrestler, that I worked hard to achieve an education over the resistance that comes with poverty. The name change meant that I would have to start over, but at the time I felt like a nobody. That is the feeling of poverty, a message of my father. 'I was no good and good for nothing,' he would say in jest, but somehow it was a message passed onto him.

"I was the oldest of six children from a mother who struggled with male relationships, in which my biological father with the Faust name and she divorced early, when I was about two years old. My father insisted at the time of my graduation that I take on his Faust name in place of 'McKee' assigned to my half brothers and sisters, the name I had used for many years. Anyway, there I was, a nobody, adjusting to a new name, crossing the stage, but starting out with the bold Faust and the alter ego, a writer's pseudonym 'Mac Keyes,' like my little partner on this journey, except you're called Ant X."

"Here I am." Ant X peered from behind the lamp touching the fish ceramic painting. "I can hardly get a word in edgewise."

"Two big stories are displayed on this wall and it depends—do you want to start from the top or not?" I pointed this out to my subjective friend even as he crawled to the frame and scanned the colorful textures of the tiles. He made the choice easier.

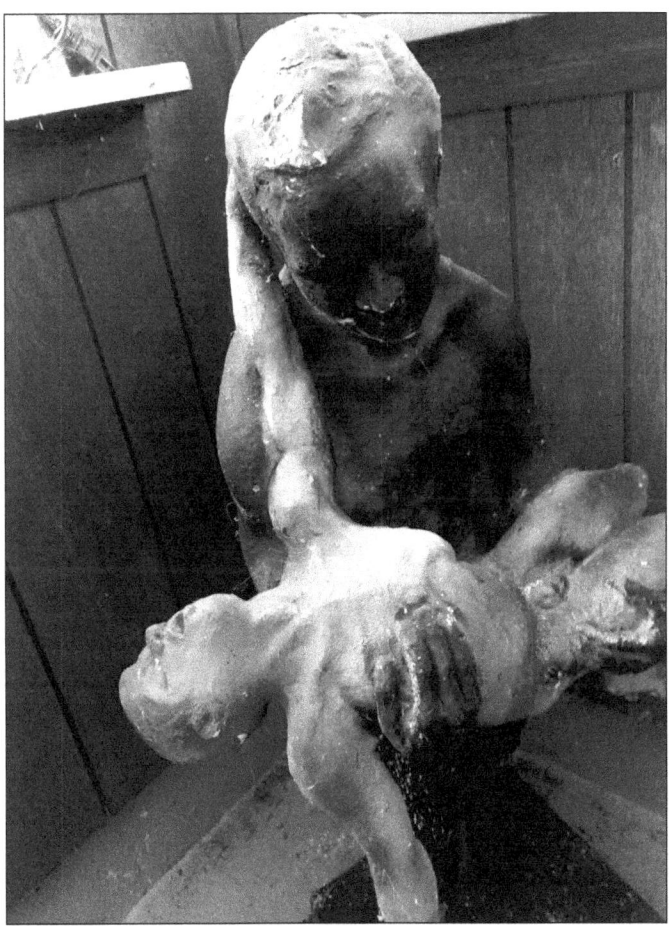

Samaritan Art from Parish

Lake of the Ozarks Parish

THE PICTURE FRAME CONSISTED of thirteen pieces of tile arranged into three interacting fishes, two blue wrapped around one red, simply entitled "Fish" by Sister Mary Leo.

Ant X studied the image with his right antenna thoughtfully dancing in the air. "Isn't that picture an old symbol for Christians?"

"That's right," I said. "And the inscription with it is a statement about the closing of leisure ministry."

"How does that begin?"

I read, "This work of art points to something that transcends simple appreciation of the work itself. It is a symbol that represents the essence of the Lake of the Ozarks Parish."

Ant X quickly asks, "What else does it say?"

"The Lake of the Ozarks Parish was 'an ecumenical ministry in re-creation and leisure.' The Parish was a record of persons who gave insight, creativity and spiritual energy during a unique history between the summer of 1965 and March 31, 1984. The Parish was a 'presence' to the vacationer, a model of leisure ministry, a ministry of alternatives, a pioneer of new breakthroughs. In every case, its essence carried the idea of 'creativity.'"

Always curious, Ant X asked, scratching his head, "What is this Leisure Ministry?"

"It was an attempt to do church that would reach out to the tourists in non-traditional ways and intersect with people on their spiritual journey," I responded, and quickly added, "persons are open to the Spirit during their leisure and play times."

"How do you define leisure?" questioned Ant X.

"In a doctorate dissertation I defined leisure as the freedom to concentrate on an activity that provided play or spiritual enrichment. It embraced the more quiet notion of meditation or the more active version of play."

"Tell me more," inquired Ant X.

"Gladly!" I responded. "It was the high point of my work in the church, since I served a local congregation on the 'Strip,' and then worked part-time as Associate Director of the Parish. My CB handle was 'Rev On the Strip.'"

"I bet that made for a lot of jokes?" Ant X was chuckling.

"I would step out my front door since the parsonage was next to the church and a sea of humanity alive with the neon lights was concentrated in the parking lot!" I held up my outstretched arms.

"It just seems like what you were doing was not traditional church," noted Ant X, studying the colorful fish on the rectangular frame.

"It wasn't. We took the church to the tourists who were visiting this 1300-mile recreational area backed up by Bagnell Dam, a playground in the middle of Missouri."

"How did it start?" asked Ant X.

"The Methodists were looking to start a new church in 1964 but soon realized that an ecumenical effort was needed that would not duplicate the usual model of another denomination. They needed something that would fit a campground setting. The Lake of the Ozarks Parish had an administrative Board of over ten denominations in a day when such cooperation worked. And that was the way it was for almost 20 years before the monies began to dry up and the churches turned ingrown and protective of local programs."

"The church must have been open to change," Ant X expounded thoughtfully.

"We were on the cutting edge." I said excitingly, "We created some 26 unique ministries to meet the needs of others even if it was just a rest on the Strip when businesses only served patrons. We were the social justice component of the lake."

"What were some of your ministries?" inquired Ant X.

"Worship was a key part of it. I remember taking the motorboat to several campgrounds and ending up at the chapel of Millstone Lodge ready to pass out bulletins and guitar in hand with special songbooks. Others took the circuit to RV campgrounds and outdoor resorts such as the Lodge of the Four Seasons.

"The VIEW program consisted of college-age young people who were responsible employees and gave 15 hours per week to leisure ministry while living a lifestyle considerate of others in the VIEW community. Volunteers In Ecumenical Witness provided energy and creativity to the summer programs and gathered during Sunday Communion to bond and refresh their faith. They stayed at the Hill Top that was used as a Retreat Center during the Off-season.

"Another program was the Treasure House that sold Christian Art and told about programs such as the Vesper Cruise on the Tom Sawyer and the coffee house called the Back Door. During this time many servicemen came to the coffee house to hear folk music and share an open mike and stay overnight at the Bunker. Interesting conversations and drama by the 11–28 Players found their way into the nooks and slides of the coffee house. It was an active meeting spot for those searching for ideas and engaging in chess and other games. This was a day that preceded loud overwhelming music and instead was a background for examining ideals.

"The Parish filled the gaps for Helpline crisis intervention, a Counseling Center and Noah's Ark child care. It tried to respond to human need with available resources and provide alternatives to dehumanizing situations. A Communiversity tried to address many justice issues but its focus on leisure ministry did not always connect the dots with peace and environmental concerns. However the Parish represented the go-to group to bring social justice to the Lake of the Ozarks area.

Ant X could hardly contain himself. Squatting high on the picture frame, he asked, "This must have been a fun time to do church?"

"Then the church wasn't so frightfully ingrown, or maybe it was because the Parish had some visionary leadership."

"Or maybe you were around fun-like folk on vacation," countered Ant X.

"True, but they carried problems with them even though they were trying to escape from those problems," I pondered.

"Escape!" interjected Ant X as he examined the next big poster. "Escape is a good leisure activity. Something I need to do on this journey without hurting myself."

"We took on difficult topics like the Vietnam war, racial discrimination, gender issues during discussions in the Back Door coffee house, Study groups and talks, but for the most part we saw escape as a healthy alternative from the pain of reality," I added. "All this is documented in a doctoral dissertation, 'A Leisure Ministry: A Study of the Lake of the Ozarks Parish and Its Impact on the Local Church.'"

"So you wrote about this unique concept of leisure ministry," said Ant X. "What did you discover?"

"That Church could be perceived differently," I added in a teachable moment, "that most people could choose church as an enjoyable leisure activity and escape from an overly indulgent Protestant Work Ethic."

"You mean that Church could become the Grand Escape from the harshness of life?" Ant X thought he was saying something profound.

"Not really, but here is a kernel of truth perhaps."

"Why did you leave if you loved this area so much?" asked Ant X.

"I didn't want to. But I became disillusioned by a forceful bully who was trying to take the church down with him, and I thought how easily the church can miss the mark and destroy the ideals of its core values, crushing innocent people who just want to be kind to one another." I pointed out, "Life can be unfair, especially for the compassionate who feel empathy for others. Also the atmosphere was politically toxic. Many avoided uncomfortable subjects."

"But I gather that there was much to take away from your experience in leisure ministry?" inquired Ant X.

"Absolutely," I said.

"What's that?" Ant X had his antennae perked up.

"A nugget of truth for me was the mantra I adapted from Gordon Dahl, 'We worship our work, work at our play and play down our worship.'" I thought over these words, realizing that we are off-balanced in our priorities and that critical thinking is an answer for our malaise.

All Ant X could mutter was, "Deep."

Theta Phi

During the closing of the Parish we distributed art pieces that celebrated this wonderful era of creativity. I received not only the Fish tile but also a sculpture "The Good Samaritan" by Sister Jean Dupree. The three-foot piece showed a strong man carrying another in obvious distress. The art was priceless in revealing the secret treasures of the many lives touched by the Parish.

Next to the Fish depiction are these words:

> Art expresses reality in images; religion expresses ultimate reality in symbols. Religious art exposes a deeper level of reality. Religious art that opens up a hidden reality does more than provide the religious content; it also digs deep for the chaos of life, below the smooth surface of living. Religious art uncovers the spiritual dimension that seems to be revealed through its images.
>
> This artistic creation reinforces the spiritual traces that kept emerging in the life of the Parish. At times the spiritual energy of the Parish was buried deep in the chaos of its institutional life but at other times a burst of energy emerged to create outstanding new programs.
>
> We would grieve the farewell of the Parish. But this work of art reminds those who were involved with the Parish that the idea of the Parish can be affirmed more strongly than ever. The memory of its creativity, its wise use of leisure, its VIEW community, its ultimate concern about meeting the needs of others is indestructible. The transforming power of the spirit lives on.

> This artistic work will find a home in a "Treasure House" of memories. Tomorrow perhaps we can rise to the surface on which we live and again express leisure ministry and creativity. By Ron Faust

I plopped myself into the beanbag cushion to wonder if these words were fortuitous to the way things were turning out in real time. It seemed like life was going backward when Congress stood in the way of progress and the world perceived the meanness of the so-called richest nation. I slumped down more in disgust as I thought about how rich people like the Koch Brothers finance billions to fight the science of climate change. The artistic works masked a hidden force that pointed to something significant but sometimes it didn't—just more chaos in the institutions.

"Sometimes it is evil," I thought.

How to make sense of this was the vulnerable question. Then I looked down at another plaque that read:

International Society of
Theta Phi

Ronald L. Faust
has been awarded membership in
the Society in consideration of scholarship
and distinction.

The plaque sports a Golden seal and signatures of the National President, National Secretary, and Chapter Representative.

"Are you confused why some words are capitalized and others are not?" asked Ant X. "Like some words seek their own self-importance."

"Interesting observation," I said, "like some references to military terms or religious figures, such as judges and ministers, often receive caps on generic words."

"This seems like a boastful practice." Ant X marched pretentiously around in circles.

I noted, "When my education degree allowed me to call myself Doctor, I rarely used the title unless I wanted to add some 'punch' to my authority."

"Maybe some intellectuals add degrees to prop up their poor self-esteem," said the Ant.

"I guess some of that was going on at the time I was moving through Seminary, but why do some receive recognition and others don't? It seems arbitrary and depends on who is around to be impressed. Or you might be in the wrong place at the wrong time, as many an innocent victim of drone warfare.

"For a moment I felt smart in the midst of all the times I have trouble figuring out this electronic age," I told Ant X.

Ant X noted, "As fate would have it, one day you are the target of an award and the next day you may be hit with a gun."

Fish Art and poster

Trifecta Resista

ANT X, WHILE I had my eyes closed, looked up at Quadrant II and saw this huge 2012 poster that reads "MidWest Trifecta Resista." In the middle is a yellow peace sign over a blue and white world with words underneath: Peace-Training-Education-Action, followed by Pace e Bene—Col. Ann Wright—Kathy Kelly, and followed again by three circles, Fort Leavenworth—NNSA Campus—Whiteman AFB.

Ant X almost fell off his perch to find a better view of the bottom list of sponsors, which included KC Peace Planters, Physicians for Social Responsibility, PeaceWorksKC, Benedictines for Peace, Sisters of Charity of Leavenworth, Vets for Peace, Loretto Peace and Justice Network, Disciples Peace Fellowship KC, American Friends Service Committee, Catholic Workers, Occupy Kansas City.

"So how did you pull this one off?" popped off Ant X.

I said, "Well, we went in cars and vans to the three sites in 2012, and in 2014, we hired a bus."

That's what we did that year. It costs a lot of money to charter a bus, but it was impressive to unload peacemakers at the resistance sites. First, in both 2012 and 2014, we went with our signs to Fort Leavenworth to advocate on behalf of Chelsea Manning.

Chelsea was an evolving story from the days of her arrest for releasing classified information to WikiLeaks, from her gender change to her need for medical treatment, from her six years in solitary confinement to her imprisonment at Fort Leavenworth.

PeaceWorks was advocating her freedom. We held up signs such as "No More Solitary for Chelsea" and "Exposing War Crimes is not a crime."

Some of the results of our protest were a letter-writing campaign in 2015–16 and a last-minute appeal to President Obama late 2016 for a pardon. PeaceWorks took a brave stance up against spurious hate speech from the other side accusing her of being a traitor. Against these odds the advocacy of PeaceWorks made a difference for Chelsea. But this was just one of the poster circles for the Trifecta Resista, a name proposed by Tamara Severns at a breakfast with peace activist Ann Wright.

We drove from Fort Leavenworth back to Kansas City for lunch, then went south in cars to the new NNSA facility on Hwy 150 and Botts Road. The site was called by various names, including CenterPoint and National Security Campus. Kansas City, Missouri, was caught up in ownership of this new Federal Facility, financed by city bonds sold to private investors. The old plant came out of WWII in 1942 and entered the bomb-making business in 1949, making the triggers that make the missiles work, plus 85% of the non-nuclear components of nuclear weapons, including the triggers that makes the bombs explode.

The problem that came to light was a substantial number of workers at the old site who were affected by the toxins that contributed to their death, in some 154 or more cases reported by families. One of the whistleblowers who opened awareness to the plight of the workers was retired supervisor Maurice Copeland. About 100 protestors were eventually arrested and went through trials and incarceration to raise awareness to the dangers of opening a new plant. Several were arrested in 2012 and 2014 during the Trifecta Resista.

When we traveled by bus to Whiteman AFB in 2014, we were featuring the downside of the use of Drones. At the time Drones were a secretive weaponry that was directed by pilotless technology, but word was out about innocent children being hit. We had protested before at Whiteman, drawing attention to the dangers of nuclear proliferation.

I settled in the beanbag and tried to recall who was arrested at Whiteman AFB. This was not the time that one of our protesters, Tamara Severns, was apprehended for trying to go to the restroom, although restroom visits were possible in previous protests. The charges against her were dropped. Whiteman always presented a challenge because the courts liked to play hardball in handing out long sentences. One such case that I will share later involved my friend who received six months of jail time when I got five years of parole.

I thought how difficult it is to be a peacemaker whenever money is involved. A wealthy right wing invests billions in offshore tax havens to secretly support candidates and the messaging protects operations like Drone technology and the fossil fuel industry. Liberal ideas are shut out by money directed toward powerful forces protecting the status quo.

Ant X called out, "I know what you are thinking. Money contaminates the political process. Sometimes money does become the root of evil when profit is made at the expense of others, and money can buy elections."

Looking at a sign close to the poster, Ant X read: "Imagine the Love we speak of made real; imagine the Peace we hope for come true; imagine it in one time, inside us and in other places."

"Is that all we can do—imagine it?" I asked.

"Maybe so, maybe so. It is a silent yearning inside many people but money seems to buy into all this noise on war," commented Ant X, climbing over seven books on a middle shelf.

These were books belonging to the author.

Bookshelves

The Books

I don't know what to say about these books because I'm not much on bragging, nor am I good at accepting another's compliment. "Anyway, Thank you, I do think they are good books."

The earliest book was *GRAND PARENTING*, coauthored with Toni Faust, who provided the inspiration for the laboratory experiment in raising our kids, Jeremy and Tuesday. We waited to write this book until we could see that they turned out all right. One never knows what the future will hold in the chaos of growing up. Each generation responds to a different set of values. And young people want to choose their own path in spite of what others might say.

The value of the book was a number of tips for Grandparents who take on the role of mentoring and share the stories of their heritage, passing on the core values of peace, justice, ecology, openness, authenticity and lots of love. Actually a revision of the book, entitled *GRAND PARENTING for Compassion and Peace*, addresses the violence in this society and how to raise peacemakers.

We wanted to teach young people how to make good choices and grow up as functioning, compassionate adults. But another generation came along that seemed to self-indulge in meeting a child's every need.

Ant X was beside himself with questions. "Did you really think you could find a formula for success?"

"Not really. We only took a risk at saying something because our own kids turned out well," I cautiously observed.

"Well, what is the answer?"

"I think a lot of it is growing up feeling that you are loved, but I wish it was more than this. I wish that more people cared about the environment and had some political savvy." I turned contemplative. "Each generation has the potential to lose its interest in peace whenever an atmosphere of hate turns violent."

One of my recent books is *Poems for Lonely Prophets*. The title reflects the solitude of unpopular positions; some of us hear the sound of a different drumbeat that questions the rationale for war. This was spelled out when a Judge ordered the protesters to write an essay on questions justifying war, such as, "What do you do with an aggressive nation if they drop the bomb first?"

"Wait, didn't the USA already do that?" popped up Ant X. "And the whole world is dealing with terminal nuclear devices and what to do with radiation."

"The bad guy is not always the other guy."

Ant X observed three poetry books called *Prophetic Poetry*. He asked, "Why so many?"

"I got into so many because poems best express some bizarre feelings, while prose attempts to be rational for an irrational justification of nuclear weapons." I said, "It was a way to break through the madness."

"Or create it!" said Ant X, looking at the pile of seven books, not mentioning three others. My play "Hindsight of a Dam Site" was performed by local actors at Lake Ozark for its 50-year celebration. Another earlier poetry book was *A Cup of Coffee* for the coffee house experience, and then another was called *Stalactites,* for some exotic intrigue.

I liked all these books, particularly the *Prophetic Poetry* volumes. Most of the poems were read at Protest marches and made a point of clarifying certain values such as Peace, Justice, Ecology, Openness, Authenticity and Love.

"Where did you come up with that?" asked Ant X, pacing back and forth on the next-to-last shelf.

"Well . . . it didn't come out of a vacuum but from core values sweeping across centuries of Biblical data and theological analysis." I paused to let that sink in.

"What do you mean?"

"It had to do with developing the ethics of how people could get along over time, not so much that an Authority said this or that, although 'Love God and Neighbor' pointed to a summary of ethical behavior," I simply said, I realized it was not that simple when I thought back on my fictional account of the search for values in the book *GAPS*.

"By the way." I said, "I used a pseudonym for that book."

"Why did you do that?" asked Ant X, revealing a little angst for asking.

"Because it alluded to some sexual innuendoes and I didn't know how people would receive the passionate parts."

"You mean it talked about sex?" Ant X shyly said.

Now here's the unbelievable part. Right when he was stunned by what he said, not wanting to be accused of sexual harassment, overcome by his insignificance of being, he teetered and tottered off a book onto the next shelf, landing on his right back leg, leaving himself immobile. He grimaced. But what was unbelievable was the rescue of a female Ant flying in from nowhere, or was he stunned in a dream-like reverie? She carefully applied a salve and wrapped his leg with a tiny, very tiny patch. Then she flew away. It was a soothing mirage. It was also a sexual fantasy. It was a love that encouraged the Ant to hobble onto his feet. It caused me to think about my latest book and how illusive love can appear.

What a relief to write about love in the book, *Five Faces of Love*. It is a book about Romance, Friendship, Caring, Justice, and Peace. What sets this book apart is the way love is separated from sex, that one can have a deep intellectual friendship without sexual activity and one can care for another without expressing sexual feeling. In the mind-field of love, one can connect the dots to many notions of love without confusing it with the culture equivalency of sex. This is a poetry book, inspiring when talking about the intimacy of love.

Ant X kept on looking for his one true love.

The Portrait

One can climb to see a Portrait of the Homecoming Queen at Eureka College on the next lower shelf by clinging to the frame, which surrounds a protrusion of sailboats and embellished anchors, at least if you are a traveling precocious ant. It's seems like a pause at a Wayside Inn to read its inscription: "This hope we have is an anchor to the soul. A hope both sure and steadfast. –Heb. 6:19."

This affirmative statement wishes for something more than the news that comes out of Egypt where ISIS claims to have caused the death of over 300 Sufis worshipping in a Mosque.

"Just wiped out like a bunch of ants with no sacred respect," said Ant X. "Same kind of thing everyday."

Ant X just sat there, broken-hearted, feeling pain in the world.

Then he looked up and saw another image showing a beautiful face of kind eyes, robust cheeks and a welcoming smile. The delicate earrings provide a nice touch to the teacher demeanor of someone you would like to meet when life goes south. This 1997 portrait crisscrossed a time when our kids went to college and my love was at the height of her teaching career. Shortly after this she moved from a second-grade school position to be a Montessori teacher, taking extra training. This also was the time we coauthored the GRAND PARENTING book, combining our ideas after experimenting with child-raising and then seeing how our kids turned out. We are proud of the experiment. One can gaze at this picture and imagine how alive she came around children and how children were prioritized to realize their best potential. Her love was the reason our children turned out well; I just provided balance and wrote books.

Our marriage was a delayed love story, told in love poetry and humor around meals. Toni would pen notes, "Hi my darling Lion Heart. I still want to be your beloved."

"I look at this picture and find hope," said I, watching the antics of Ant X, who was hanging from a balance bar of a ball and golf figure. Toni and I both liked to play golf since it was a game we could do together without keeping score.

A picture on the same shelf, showing our daughter and her handsome husband, was a reminder of how important the arts were for a balanced life. Both were into the arts, she into dance and he into paintings whenever he wasn't white-water rafting. This picture provided a double dose of hope that drew attention away from the malaise of life.

Another cube shows a picture of our son holding his French horn. He made us feel proud with his bountiful energy and ability to take responsibility. I would often say, "How could we be so lucky! How did this thoughtful person gift us with his magical presence, always willing to host a family Birthday?" He was always willing to help and threw himself into many home projects.

Ant X was dreamily engaged in an image of being happily wedded in a mixed marriage. It's difficult to generalize about the complex reproductive life of an ant. Sometimes there are more queens settled in a colony. Sometimes there are so many species that the genes get mixed up, defying patterns. The life of an ant starts from an egg, which if fertilized will become a female. If not, it will be a male. The larva goes through a pupal stage before emerging as an adult and workers regurgitate food of seeds and meat in liquid form out of a social stomach. Sometimes female-breeding workers other than Queens emerge as adults, and other times male drones come into play. Ant X represented a minority group of many varieties. Besides, he was a Drone, easily detectable as a foreigner to many colonies. He was a marked ant susceptible to being killed. But he also wanted to be with the Queen at great risk to his well-being.

"So what's happening?"

"Nothing much," Ant X casually replied.

"Nothing?"

"Well, I'm actually bothered by the notion that racism is so pervasive, that some feel uncomfortable about looking different," said the tiny ant, knowing that he was different.

"At least you are not a white nationalist."

"What does that mean?" Ant X asked.

It was a phrase I heard from the radio on "Democracy Now," in which the main problem of a Trumpo world was identified as white nationalism. A group of white males are trying to defend an old way of life and become fearful of those who are different. Their power is centered in a patriotic zeal for country, war and guns. They have no room for minority groups; they hate these groups.

Bully blustery types who are afraid of losing power often ostracize minorities.

"Sad, isn't it?" I asked Ant X.

"The most insignificant things keep people apart, silly stuff, the way people behave or look. Ants too!" exclaimed Ant X.

"Some of the problem in human behavior is the rigidity with control issues. People cannot let go of their need to manage the outcome; they are insistent on doing it their way," surmised the philosopher in me. "If only they could just be more tolerant and ignore the little stuff that doesn't amount to anything."

"I'm for taking a step back, shedding some ego feathers and letting others live out their lives." Ant X crossed his legs and wished he had a joint to smoke like some other ants he admired during rest.

"I think it has a lot to do with legal issues—whether one is following what is right or wrong," I added. "Some only obey Rules and Regulations and are uncomfortable with ambiguous situations, which is the way life mostly is, more greys than black or white choices."

"Whom would you rather be with? People who are prickly stern or goosey nurturing in having fun?" queried Ant X.

"I would prefer the latter but might like the former if they were piloting a plane I was flying," I said.

"I think it is the way you think. That's key," said Ant X. "Thinking has a lot to say about control. Since most do not want to be out of control, they maintain this façade that everything is okay. We go around living these lives of insignificance trying to pretend that we are someone other than who we are. We become camouflaged persons hiding our true selves. Sad!" As if an ant could arrive at this mature thought, except that frequently the better viewpoint comes from minority positions.

"Where in life can we find an answer?" I posed.

"Authenticity."

That was a word that came to mind when I looked at the outer Portrait of the hidden presence of my young wife, smiling with her kind eyes.

Higher Levels

LEAPING AND BOUNDING OVER the second shelf to reach the top shelf, like fingers flipping through the yellow pages, Ant X passed by the books that inspired a lifetime of higher education. Those who disparage education cannot see the hours poured over valuable writings to assimilate the material and allow the thoughts to seep into the marrow of one's bones but that is what it takes to integrate the best thinking, to absorb a lifetime of learning. One of the most useful books was Abraham Maslow's *The Farthest Reaches of Human Nature* with insights into the Hierarchy of Needs in Motivation and Personality, whereby one can rise above survival needs and search for higher needs through respect and ultimately authenticity. A similar evolving was presented in a book by James Fowler, *Stages of Faith*, advancing faith beyond imagination and literal understanding toward a questioning faith and a self-integrative faith. Higher education brought a welcomed understanding of a more mature faith and its implication for social justice. This book displayed insights concerning social justice rather than quick schemes to secure a place in Heaven.

My discovery of the theologian Paul Tillich had a most profound impact on me. *The Courage To Be* and *The New Being* captured the essential nature of existence with Platonic language that was exciting and sustainable. Another theologian that made a difference to me was Reinhold Niebuhr, who opened up an understanding of sin as sensuality or pride, showing in his *Moral Man and Immoral Society* how slow society is to find a moral centeredness,

Higher Levels

measured by justice. There was Process Theology, there was Hans Kung, *On Being a Christian,* there were all kinds of counseling books, particularly one by my mentors Lowell Colston and Paul Johnson, writing *Personality and Christian Faith.* So many books! So many learnngs! So many hours of allowing ideas to flood the soul with knowledge. Then to leave this shelf to risk a new shelf.

The next shelf was higher up in the sense of taking social justice issues to another level, a level of peace studies. Ant X was running back and forth on this shelf while noticing books about racial justice, confronting the existence of a group feeling superior or dominant over another. Justice themes include not only the black experience but also the phenomenon of poverty and the indigenous American. You would think that racial relationships would be further along but that seems not to be the case. The trouble is that we inherit a society that separates people by color, cash and company, maybe even more so by association with conservatives or liberals. Breaking through these tensions is the work of peace.

"I always thought the work of peace was a higher activity requiring a vision that would help us survive and move away from war," I suggested. "Peace required safety, a space where we could coexist, where we would want to be together more than pulled apart at the seams."

"Well then, why is that so hard? asked Ant X.

"I don't think it would have to be, if we could tolerate the small stuff and let go of the crevices, such as when you look at the blue planet Earth and crunch your eyes and melt the demarcations into a fluid melting pot."

"You mean meditate yourself into oneness?" wondered Ant X.

"Something like that," I paused, "or at least develop more empathy toward others and think that one is no better than anyone else."

"Really?"

"But where is the significance in all that?" I asked.

"There isn't any. All of us are insignificant together. Merely ants doing our tasks," said Ant X, tweaking his antenna.

"What if our significance comes by celebrating our insignificance!"

"How does that work?" wondered the tiny ant.

"I don't think we are finished with our story yet."

"Then maybe we can create our future rather than destroy it!" sputtered Ant X.

Creation

"So what's happening, Little Creature?" I asked.

"Nothing much," came the reply.

"Maybe you're pacing back and forth to stay out of the rain," I noted.

Ant X twitched a bit. "There you go, as Ants go marching one by one, Hoorah, Hoorah."

What I like about arriving in this shelf of Quadrant II is a focus on Creation, which grounds us in the wonder of what is there, which connects us to reality through our senses, which leads us to experience confirmation of scientific theories. This shelf cradles a guide to American Trees, another on Stars and a third on Fish. You would think that observation of the world around us would offer universal communication by which to construct our future and enjoy its transcendent dimensions, but rather it often provides escape from reality. Many design elaborate conspiracy theories that deaden the pain of existence and take one into exciting flights of fancy.

Many look to cinema for feeling intense fear, perhaps from a Hitchcock thriller. Others are drawn into Harry Potter epics that offer make-believe distortions of characters and scenery. Some others show sentimentality, playing off child-like emotions for Teddy Bear objects of comfort. Life can be hard; entertainment can ease the pain.

You would think most of us would want to protect the environment in the only planet we know. Somehow a destructive streak contaminates the human condition and erases what progress we have made.

A good example of the resistance to climate change is Congress's denial of the scientific data showing human activity has increased carbon dioxide in the atmosphere, leading to the rise of sea levels. The GOP sides up with the fossil fuel industry, which is making as much money as possible and ignoring climate change. Neither the party nor the industry will take responsibility for fossil fuel's negative impact. It seems to be in the DNA of the GOP to pick up the "con" of Congress and be against progress.

Ant X pipes up, "Did you see the sign in the Room that read, 'No Tea for Me, Thanks. I Prefer Progress'?"

Actually and theologically, it's a sin to be against progress. Niebuhr understands sin in two ways, as the sin of sensuality and the sin of pride. The sin of sensuality misses the mark at the physical point of degrading another sexually. In the sin of pride, people think that they are far more important than who they actually are. Both sins present a false image of one's authentic humanity. A third sin doesn't show up in Niebuhr's work; it fails to act on its potential—what we might call the sin of omission.

Those who miss an opportunity to move forward or who block progress by deliberately scuttling the process engage in sin. I say this without trying to be judgmental; those who move backwards are deceiving themselves if they think there are no consequences. Conservatives who rigidly hold onto the past and delight in frustrating liberals have reason to wonder whom they hurt and what regression they support.

Some start off with flawed assumptions that we live in a dog-eat-dog world where the competition is fierce and only a few survive. This Darwinian notion of survival of the fittest means that all persons are on their own, picking themselves up by their bootstraps and leaving the weak behind. This promotes a selfish individualism and prevents a nurturing social concern. This defends mean-spirited attitudes that throw people out on the street or, for example, toss people off their health care. This does not promote a humane, compassionate society.

CREATION

The addiction to money seems to be the single most important factor in destroying this earth. Some give up their principles for keeping fossil fuels in the ground, for trading in gas-guzzling automobiles, for finding jobs that produce alternative energy. Many have no compulsions about working for uranium-based companies or military contractors dealing with toxic materials. The idea is to acquire a good-paying job without asking about the product or raising questions about any secret national defense project. A successful job measures a high salary more than the worth of the product, whether it benefits humankind or not.

Ant X was climbing down to the next shelf by crawling underneath the shelf and free falling onto a prehistoric rock carved out to expose a crystal wall surrounding a toy dinosaur creature, almost as small as a one-inch ant. Ant X landed on top of the geode but gained a perspective of longevity, that is to say, how long it takes to form a geode but how brief is the life span of humans. I guess it doesn't seem that brief at the time until one experiences how the weeks hastily go by. Humans trick themselves into believing that filling their schedule with unimportant things will make their lives significant. What really fills up the time is worry. The mind repeats scenes of what to wear, what to say, and what could go wrong.

Nobody suspects that these mind games are rehearsed over and over again because we lie to ourselves, even perpetuating the lie to others. When someone asks how we are doing we automatically say, "Fine," not wanting to get into a long conversation about how "unfine" we feel, about the enormous amount of time we are worrying about our next meeting. The parallels between human activity and ant colonies are uncanny as both societies scurry over the earth or in work places, gathering food and cleaning utensils and throwing away trash—ad nauseam tasks that preoccupy minutes and moments until the time is displaced by mindless thinking about nothing.

Ant X turned to me with a silly ant's grin. "Thus we age. Thus we rot. Thus we waste time. Thus we fight for the privilege to do so. We treasure our insignificance."

"But we tend to stay that way, stuck, because we are not curious enough to learn anything different," I moaned. "We stay uneducated."

"I have a hard time accepting the failure to connect ethics with certain political issues," said Ant X, squinting to invite darkness.

"You'll find some of the finest Christian folk, so they claim, with some of the most hateful positions," I observed.

"It's like they feel most comfortable living in the dark, less threatened, but actually it's most scary." The tiny ant closed his eyes again.

"What do you mean?"

Ant X went on, "I'm disturbed that so much is destroyed without any concern for the environment. One report says that the corporation Bayer was producing pesticides that were taking out 75% of the Bees that pollenate plant life. Or what about Monsanto using pesticides that unfortunately kill milkweed that is life-support for Butterflies?"

"Unbelievable," I said, alarmed.

"Mass extermination of certain species!" said Ant X, who was well aware he was part of a million ants for every human.

"But what is my future since pesticides are extinguishing all these Bees?" he wondered.

"Call it an 'Insect Apocalypse.'"

Deception

ANT X WASN'T DOING well. His demise was weighing heavily on him. He feared that any minute some human shoe would squash him. He was still feeling pain from the previous fall in which he had a near-death experience with visions and delusional episodes. Something hit him that set off sharp pains from pressure in his lower stomach where he stored food. He was pacing near the edge of the shelf to alleviate the ache when he found himself falling and landing on the video called "Betrayal," about an attack on Pastors by persons called "Clergy Killers."

You would think that the last place you would find deception would be in the church where a community of nice people bolster the nice ministry of a nice shepherd who cares for his or her flock serving a nice God. What makes this unrealistic is the use of the word "nice." It borders on hypocrisy.

Maybe the deception starts at the top. One assumes that God is always good until one asks questions why a nice God allows the holocaust to visit an innocent people or, for that matter, permits any disaster that causes mass extermination. Could a nice God stand aloof in the midst of torture to teach the victim a lesson in perseverance or to establish a mysterious plan? Would a nice capricious God make a point of showing us free will and punish us when we make the wrong choice? When life has been unfair it is no wonder that we have some angry folk who display their frustration on God's representative—the Clergy.

If the answer is that we cannot understand the mysteries of the universe and are not supposed to question the wisdom of God, then where is a legitimate place to have this argument? It simply is a matter of accepting some things on faith.

Teeny Ant X just lay there, on top of the disk "Betrayal," not like he was Bug Splat, but close, feeling betrayed, with sharp streaks piercing his teeny body, mortified and helpless. He lay prone on his back with his bottom two legs crossed to numb the pain and his upper antennae flinging wildly and quixotically. Just thinking . . . maybe not much of anything, wondering if he were dead or alive. He thought how easy it would be to check out of life, losing all his testosterone to keep his species going. At this moment he had no Queenie, no God, no reason to live, not yet, unless he could wait to manufacture some grand scheme, maybe a conspiracy theory, why he should take another breath—actually all he could do was be still.

It would be inconsequential if someone with a big boot came by and stepped on him. Gone. Skip the misery, the worry, the wasting away of time, wondering if there was more than nothing. But then one could laugh about the existential dilemma of being an ant and certainly that of being human. Humans have been betrayed by a cruel joke, that we expected something when there is really nothing. It turns out that something in the human psyche needs to find meaning in taking up space.

Some are able to do this better than others, that is, accept things. You either destroy or create; that is the way it is, go on. So when I was a clergyman my biggest difficulty was how many small-minded people were missing the big picture since they did not care about a vision for peace, or getting in there to work against injustices, or becoming stewards of the earth with a sensitivity for ecology. They just wanted to be taken care of and have a place to feel comfortable with their friends. I noticed that during prayer time, the number one requests concerned the hospital and physical well-being of the members rather than loss from disasters around the world. The Biblical connection with a higher vision is a low priority for the average layperson, so any controversy in the church meant that the preacher was on the firing line as an obvious casualty. Intuitive types are considered separated from reality, and the higher concerns are to be practical and take care of the building and keep within the budget. In other words, it is valuable to be conservative and conserve what you got.

Faith allows for doubt that questions certain assumptions of a belief system of the church; why would you need faith if the answers were all secure? I think it is possible to be a participant of the church and raise questions about the attributes of God, such as referring to God as Peace or Creator or Love, which generally are accurate references. What about seeing faith as an admittance of wonder and mystery without assigning the term God to Jesus, maybe just Peace or Spirit or Christ, making them interchangeable?

The significance of the human being is the Being dimension, the Spiritual part, while the human part is physical, such as the parallel to Jesus or the body of God referring to the world. Interchangeable are the dimensions of human, physical, Jesus, world, bread held in juxtaposition with Being, Spirit, Christ, Energy and Wine. Interesting theology, don't you think? The combination of physical dimensions becomes significant with the Spirit, otherwise it dies in insignificance.

The deception is that we can get along without recognizing the Spirit. Most of the time we proceed by simply checking the battery on our phones or measuring the light source on our solar panels to conduct electricity. The energy is abundantly available if we tap into its power source, but it finds religious expression when we pause and find awe in how it works.

Thus, life lives and dies, while not every death needs an answer; it happens. Do you have to say that it's God's will? Not really, if that doesn't make sense in that moment. Does that mean that the person is set to go to Heaven? Maybe there are other ways to think about that more meaningfully. One can revisit that answer later. And maybe, in the whole scheme of things what is significant to our insignificant lives has surprising answers that we haven't thought of at the time of an obituary.

I have yet to see a bit of light in my dark hour. How much money I make is not the light I'm looking for. I feel nothing when an antagonist tells me how good he feels when his 401(k) goes up. I feel it going dark when the tax code favors the rich and America's biggest resource is weapon deals. Money. Money. Money. It seems like a way to accomplish some nasty stuff. The perception that money is the only significant way to have power would make one think that money is the root of evil. Too many times it seems to be. But it can do some good, too. I just think that Jesus left us with an alternative priority.

> . . . to the least of these . . .
> . . . love the poor . . .
> . . . not be like the hypocrites . . .
> . . . you will know them by their fruits . . .
> . . . side up with the insignificant . . .

Ant X blurted out, "I almost think that if Jesus were to say anything, it would be 'Gather the teeny Ants under my care and get your marching orders to go to work by finding your play through worship.'"

Song Liturgy

ANT X AND I moved along in our journey to a most difficult subject, as I first come across a stack of song books and Hymnals. These source materials enrich the lyrical life of those raised in the church. Finding the right words to fit the occasion was always a challenge for leaders wanting to say something fresh and personal. Meanwhile I'm looking at another stack of liturgical resources and then another for special occasions, but more about that later.

Back to the song books, I guess the value of the Sunday morning ritual is that you can participate somehow by singing, by litany, by communion. It all seems like poetry or song that vibrates the human soul. A worship service permits one to continue to sing for a lifetime of enjoyment even when one feels unconfident around music.

Some great songs contribute to the DNA reservoir of religious, emotional depth. It's what becomes our tradition and what raises our spirit. It's a unifying force that shapes community and speaks volumes through a common message. Picking songs from the *Chalice Hymnal*, I resonate to the following list:

> Are Ye Able Said the Master (621)
> Faith of our Fathers (625)
> Great Is Thy Faithfulness (86)
> This Is My Father's World (59)
> In Christ There Is No East or West (687)
> Were You There? (198)
> He Lives (26)

Blessed Assurance (543)
Just a Closer Walk (557)
To God Be the Glory (70)
Be Thou My Vision (595)
Let Us Break Bread Together (425)
I Got Peace Like a River (530)
We Shall Overcome (630)
Pass It On (477)
Let There Be Peace On Earth (677)

That last song has followed me all my life and has always brought a smile to my face, although I never knew whether to sing it with an "us" or a "me."

This list of the Sweet Sixteen is admittedly sentimental but robust from the energy of each song. Music perks up the spirit and does not have to come from a Hymnal. It might be romantic like the Karen Carpenter song "Close To You" or some background support like Anne Trenning's piano music.

I generally prefer classical music over Hard Rock (I delve into that when it doesn't overwhelm me and demand unwanted attention). I used to run a coffee house in which thoughtful guitar music provided nice easy space for thinking before performance-oriented music blew out one's eardrums. Actually I like instrumental music when I'm writing because then I don't have to think of the words as extraneous noise.

"How you doin', Little Fella?" I asked while fiddling with a headset that I was trying to get to work.

"Oh, I'm all right, but I'm in a little funk," Ant X responded.

"What seems to be the matter?" I said, somewhat disinterested since I was experiencing temporary writer's block and had no song to sing.

"I'm lonely."

"Maybe you need recharging like this battery." I was hoping to use this head set to block out the noise from barking dogs, the Parks Department chain sawing of perfectly good trees except that they were in the way, and my neighbor's predictable lawn mowing.

But the tiny light was not coming on when I plugged the head set into the computer. "Why do I spend an enormous amount of time trying to make some things work?" I asked. "It makes me go crazy. I wonder why a thousand of your ant friends couldn't line up on the shelf with you and start to crawl into this input hole and magically connect some wires so that I might learn if this wireless gizmo works," I pleaded.

"It sounds like a plea to stop old age since all electronic devices baffle you," popped off Ant X annoyingly.

"I'm just going to wait for the Ant army to restore civility in the cursing of my predicament."

"I'm going to let go of this thought and go rest," murmured Ant X, scaling the nearby shelf and then passing the Sony Boom Box used for playing cassette tapes and listening to "Democracy Now" with Amy Goodman, courtesy of community radio. Ant X paused to scan the stack of tapes. He wanted to hear the sounds in "Prelude to Lazaris," "Spirit Wind," "Storms Thunder and Rain," "Gentle and Relaxing Spirit," and "No Easy Walk to Freedom" by Peter Paul and Mary. Much more; it seems one could listen forever. The Ant retreated with a sleepy yawn and plugged in his own ear bugs to listen to some quiet music.

People ask me where I go to find my news source and they give me blank stares when I tell them, "Democracy Now." Mainstream news is a TV wasteland of drivel providing the latest murder rate, the weather report and upcoming sports. When I tell them Amy Goodman is a top-rate reporter who goes into areas most reporters would not consider and uncovers the rare opposite point of view, they act clueless. She presents segments that allow time to detail the full story, prompting, "Can you talk about that?" She is a true journalist, honest, intelligent, balanced while digging for the truth. My weekday ritual is to listen to Amy & Company at 8 am on 90.1 FM in Kansas City lying in my beanbag, and then I'm ready to meet the world as a Global Citizen. I am always perplexed that people I know do not accept this daily exercise of being informed. They risk becoming close-minded, fearful and nationalistic. "O Diddily

Squat!" I told myself. "I love Amy Goodman and her reporting! Especially in a Trump era of fake news."

Life is grim. The suffering that people have to endure from uncompassionate politicians is phenomenal, but that seems to be the way the victims and oppressors accept their roles, sometimes in small doses of grim griminess. Humans and ants are so much alike, vulnerably down in the dirt. Listening to Amy helps me to remember the suffering of humanity and, hopefully, to care. It is so easy to forget. That comes out of a framework of forgetting. Most people are into getting, into taking care of their own needs, when their lives would be more significant by "giving." In every way, more forgiving and less for "getting."

I don't know why I kept these binders full of worship services as a reminder of the Sunday-by-Sunday litany. I was always searching for the right word or song to fit the occasion. It always took time to get it right because it was a theme, pulling emotion toward a Eucharistic crescendo. The early elements of worship, i.e., the synaxis (the word for the first part of the liturgy) and the actual Communion are important to know from both historical and exegesis standpoints. The art of worship requires an intuition and maturity of style to provide the words of faith, with liberal support of peace, justice and ecology, padded with wonder at creation and support of the poor. Just as a menu provides a diet of nourishment for the body, a worship service offers nourishment for the soul. Assembling bulletins in binders kept a record of moments of inspiration, even though they were moments in the past that were rarely retrieved, just like a good meal or good sex, captured only for that moment.

Some settings make a difference for good worship, such as outside at the Lake of the Ozarks. Also, borrowing words from Ann Weems, a United Church of Christ contributor, or from Ruth C. Duck in *Flames of the Spirit,* a certain setting can spark words to come alive with fresh meaning. Sometimes creating new words feeds the synergy of the group. This formation of community is more than a haphazard patchwork of words or an exercise in boredom but a real live birth to something new about life over death.

Song Liturgy

Then, in Quadrant II, to the right of this stack of liturgy are the resources for marriage and funeral celebrations. And they are celebrations of certain passages that change one's status and make life worth living. The art of liturgy is a work in progress that needs to be thoughtful and intentional to rise above the insignificant.

"Maybe you got a bit mixed up here," suggested the Ant, high on the shelf from his superior vantage point. "The bulletins were never meant to be a product."

"What do you mean?" I looked puzzled.

"Life is only temporary," the Ant stated in few words with a matter-of-fact shrug.

"Nothing is permanent, I know, I know, but that's what makes it significant," I insisted.

"Well. What are you saying?"

"The temporary things are the important things. We yearn for sex and Poof—it disappears!" I said, surprising myself. "Such a desirable come-on and then it's gone. Look at love. Quickly a kiss; then gone. Glance at the obituaries this morning. Some are so young and so quickly gone."

"It's true of every worship experience as you prepare a strand of liturgical yarn only to have it wind up unraveled and basically forgotten," offered the Ant, in his wisdom.

"It's true of the arts when it comes to theatre, Live and spectacular, in the moment, but wave upon wave, it soon disappears," I said. "So what's the learning here?" Answering myself, I pondered, "Perhaps what we desire are the insignificant, treasures that seem to be out of our reach except for special occasions," I pondered.

"I think it lasts more in songs and settles in long-term memory," admitted the Ant. "That's why I cannot erase certain ditties from my head, 'The Ants go marching two by two, Hoorah, Hoorah.'"

The Barrel

The career of ministry is probably the most insignificant job in the hemisphere, useless and ignoble and awkward to explain.

"Do you dare?" asked the Ant.

"Let's start with the Barrel, My Sermons."

The Barrel

The art of preaching was always an unusual occupation for me. I was extremely shy from childhood and fearful that I would be thrown in front of people and forget what I was going to say. That was a nightmare for me. I was always amazed that I could accomplish such a dreadful activity and, with some success, lean into my fears. The first time I had an opportunity to deliver a sermon at my home church in Vancouver, I tried to memorize it and ran into a memory block, so I tried to avoid this experience of raw panic the rest of my life. I admired preachers who could memorize but this did not play to my strengths. However, I was of the opinion that my sermons had more depth than some lackadaisical deliveries, although my sermons looked like they were naturally and freely delivered.

Through the years I learned different techniques for attempting the art of preaching. Early on I started to write my sermons on a 5" by 8" piece of paper that would fit inside a 6" by 9" church bulletin that was a similar size to many paperbound books. That way I could slip the sermon inside my bulletin or Bible and deliver it almost as if I were extemporaneously and conversationally free of rigid adherence to the written word.

A shift took place in my lifetime as a preacher. In undergraduate school we learned to compile a sermon by constructing a single focused proposition. This statement was backed up by three points and an introduction and a conclusion; each of the five components had an illustration. The key point or proposition was repeated so that the audience was reinforced with what they thought they heard. Here's the problem: the sermon could become tediously prolonged and authoritative.

Well-known homiletic professor Fred Craddock came on the scene with provocative books like *Overhearing the Gospel*. His thesis was that we were tantalized by gossip such that we could weave a narrative that would intrigue our congregations. We could allow the audience to overhear the preacher's struggle with difficult passages, and it was permissible to entertain doubt about what they heard, in scripture. In fact, the element of surprise was desirable, such that the "loop" or story was told with humor and imagination and many times was left incomplete. The audience's task was to finish the sermon. I always felt that I was respecting the brainpower of the audience. It was the task of the sermon to raise questions to sort out the ambiguity of the story line, but maybe I was assuming too much for a single-point sermon. I just preferred the drama of unfolding the story rather than pounding the gospel like a hammer on top of people's heads.

Boom. I sank into the beanbag chair and stiffened into a prickly ball, wondering what Houdini escape the Prez will use to throw off any trace of his "Fire and Fury" escapades. The book is out. Michael Wolff has made the media rounds. There seems to be unanimous agreement that the Prez may be unfit to hold this office, and yet his loyalists are going down with the ship. How can that be?

"The only thing I can figure out is that the followers of Trump justify their support as a defense of their ego, never admitting that they could be wrong, just like Trump," said Ant X, looking at the ceiling.

How can an entire party be so dishonest? They will use coded language to smile and pretend that they are a bunch of nice people, congenial and doing the work of government, but then will turn so mean-spirited, against health care, against immigration, against regulations, against climate change, against the Paris climate agreement, against Cuban normalization, against the Poor People's Campaign, against so many things. The hypocrisy drips off the words from politicians who are trying to con us into believing that they are working for the public good when in fact they are stopping forward progress. Then another book shows up, *It's Even Worse Than You Think: What the Trump Administration Is Doing to America*, by David Cay Johnston.

I know. I know. That's why I slump in this beanbag and feel this fog of gray that creeps into my psyche and turns the future dark. What words would uplift in times like these and not feel hollow and irrelevant?

What sermon would I pull out to speak of the sin of sensuality as women are courageously countering sexual harassment?

And what sermon would emerge to deal with the sin of pride that would falsely rank one group as superior to another? Racism is mixed in the fabric of America because many want to control others. But the sin that I'm talking about has to do with the sin of omission, i.e., not doing anything. Sometimes we are simply lazy and miss opportunities to move the human enterprise forward. Sometimes we are too late to seize the right words for change.

The Ant was agitated by the clutter in the Room and blurted out, "I need a vacation from traipsing around this messy Room while you are moping in a beanbag while the State of the Union is floundering."

"Where will you go?"

"Even though I act like I'm alone, I actually have many friends, some of whom I would like to see now," said Ant X, storing a tiny backpack of food. "I'm headed for one of my societies to hibernate for the winter."

I pulled out the drawer that had a magnetized figure of a lion and lamb lying together while I acknowledged the Ant's presence, "I'll see you later." Blink, he was gone.

The Barrel was the whole reason for this Room, but since I retired a decade ago I had not opened the Barrel. I always thought I would make use of these sermons at some interim ministry but never had any more desire to preach. I could write books but not preach. I didn't feel the same about it. I think my theology had changed too radically and I could no longer hide my quarrel with the Church. That's a strange thing to say since I currently support three churches.

All three are mainline churches. This means to me that they are ecumenical or will cooperate with other faith beliefs. All three would be considered liberal. I like Bethel United Church of Christ because the liturgy mentions justice as a key ingredient and my family is involved in music director and choir positions. I have been a longtime member of Community Christian Church because the Disciples of Christ offer Communion each Sunday. And I like the All Souls Unitarian Universalist Church because I like being around liberals and creative thinkers with strong stances against war and weapons. These churches provide a balanced meal to my religious diet.

I dipped into the Barrel. So many times I allowed my fingers to walk through this collection that gathered my treasure of thought, freely given and barely worth two cents, except that the Barrel held the weekly in-and-out exercise of sermonic labor, wondering what I would come up with next, if anything, except the surprise that new ideas would keep showing up.

The first section I came to was Leisure-Related Preaching. I had developed a theology of leisure that fit the church's exercise of Sunday morning activity and the casual campground settings. During the summer I would turn to light-hearted sermons such as "Fear and Faith." It would start out, "One of the most interesting incidents of scripture involves the story of the stormy sea. Seeing Jesus on the water, the disciples yell out, 'It is a ghost!' The scripture says, 'They cried out in fear.' All of us know how fear triggers our survival response. I remember when I was leading youth up the highest mountain in Colorado, Mount Elbert, 14,433 feet high, when a storm shot out lightening rods of static electricity, springing out of the soles of our shoes. We were scared but remarkably never feeling more alive." This scripture in Matthew 14:22–33 allowed one to say, "Fear destroys; faith allows us to change and grow. In fact, we would not need faith if we had the future all figured out. In the face of our fears, we might hear Jesus say to us, 'Take heart, it is I; have no fear.' When the world is changing as much as the uncertain waters beneath our feet, can we face our fears to come alive to the present moment, and decide which way it will be: fear or faith?"

Ant X mosied back, shivering from the cold. I tried to cheer him up.

I told him I always liked the title of a sermon based on Zacchaeus in Luke 19:1–10, "Up a Tree." I often used a brainteaser about a man who rides an elevator to work but gets off on the 9th floor to walk stairs to the 13th. Why? Because he was too short to reach the 13th. This was a way to introduce the notion that bigness, like authority, wealth and power, is not always better according to a little book, *Small Is Beautiful*, by E.F. Schumacher, who suggests that people are most human in smaller social units. He pleads for a different order of values, to look up from the smallness of our creatureliness and hear the voice that says, 'I must come and stay with you today,' to learn how to be a giver rather than a taker, to say with Henry Van Dyke: "Be glad of life because it gives you the chance to love and to work and to play and to look at the stars."

"I think that last sermon is one that would fit my small size," pointed out Ant X, while using his antenna like an index finger. "Really, I just want to have fun."

Once I did a sermon that gave permission to play. It expresses the problem that we worship our work, work at our play, and play down our worship. In Luke 14:15-24 a man invited his friends to a banquet but they couldn't come because they had too much work to do. I talked much about the need for a Sabbath principle, representing a rendezvous of communion with God who was the ordering principle to pace the other six days. Abraham Heschel affirmed that the Sabbath was given to us by "God for joy, for delight, for rest, so that all that is divine in the world is brought into union with God." I added that my Sabbath comes on a sailboat when I take the "Sabbatical" out on the lake. Here as I look up into the luffing sails I realize that I am most dependent upon the wind in order to move forward. I rely on something extra, the "pneuma" as an invisible spirit that turns recreation into "re-creation," and thus at play I am reenergized.

Probably one of the best scriptures to capture the insignificance of life is Ecclesiastes in such passages as Chapter 3:1-2, 7b-13, presented in the sermon "Time for All Seasons." The third chapter of Ecclesiastes catches us up in a pendulum of time; there is that tick, tock rhythm that flows through seven verses: " . . . a time to be born, and a time to die . . . a time to remember and a time to go forward . . . for everything there is a season." Then we are hit with the troubling question, "What gain has the worker from his toil?"

Life seems pretty empty at times, and all the energy expended on projects seems to be in vain. Everything seems so temporal, even those things that should last forever. Since things don't last forever that puts even more value on whatever we desire. We want it even more since it might go out of existence. So we set our sights on the temporal insignificant moments and try to string enough of these moments together. We try to make sense of verse 11: "He has made everything beautiful in its own time," as if we could find the perfect time to capture a beautiful moment to discover the rhythm, the cadences, the dance of life, to be able to experience "eternity" in its ordinariness, to realize when humans are touched by eternity, that "he has put eternity into man's mind."

"Frankly, you must rely on a good delivery so that all this talk about leisure, silence, meditation doesn't put the audience to sleep," said Ant X, sarcastically.

A quote from "Catch the New Wind" says, "He came in a certain time and a certain place. With love that could not be contained in a given time at a given place. He came in one season—for all seasons. He died one death for all deaths." He came that we might have life—and have it more abundantly. Which is about the same flow as Matthew 11:28: "Come to me, all who labor and are heavy laden, and I will give you rest. Take my yoke upon you, and learn from me; for I am gentle and lowly in heart, and you will find rest for your souls. For my yoke is easy, and my burden is light." So the one who is inconspicuous, who is lowly in status, who is the insignificant servant of others rises to significance.

"Does the next sample have more social action in it?" asked Ant X.

Through the years I came up with many sermons on the environment because it was a way to introduce social activism and elevate a respect for creation. Thus surfaced a provocative sermon, "Ecology of the Body." A most attractive phrase goes like this: "The Earth has music for those who listen . . . " It brought my attention to a series of posters, one of which says, "The mutual dependence of all creation is in each astonishing living thing." We are reminded that the wonder of creation finds everything centered in the living Christ, that it is the Christ that holds the universe together. Thus, it leads us to say that as we participate in the world, we are in effect saying something more about the way we respect Christ, or Spirit, as we honor and care for the environment.

I am intrigued by the possibility that as we look at the universe, we may be looking at God's body. Just by what we see and experience we come into contact with the evidence of God. Then too, God is still more than what we experience by our five senses. God is a spiritual power that binds each of us to look not only out there, but within us and beyond us: God relates with us at every level of existence.

Now the scriptures in Romans 12:3–8 are an important reinforcement of this notion of Christ's body in vs. 4–5. On the one hand, we are one Body, united together, but on the other hand, we find different levels of potential working together—the parts of the whole are different functions on the body of Christ. Using the analogy of a physical body, which part comes closest to depicting our own role? A hand (sharing)? An ear (listening)? A tongue (talking)? The Heart (feeling and caring)?

Matthew 5:48, "You, therefore, must be perfect, as your Heavenly Father is perfect," is an urging to reach attainment of certain stages of accomplishment in order to open up to other stages such that life is a constant changing and growing process of discovery how we fit into this universe and become aware how God breathes into this creation.

Maria Montessori, an educator of preschoolers, alludes to the need to be sensitive to our environment: "It is true that men (humans) have created enjoyments in social life and have brought about a vigorous human life in community life. But nevertheless he still belongs to nature, and especially when he is a child, he must absorb from it the forces necessary to development of the body and spirit. We have intimate communion with nature, which influences the growth of the body."

Ecology is the interaction of an organism with the environment. Montessori believes in providing a learning environment that would reveal and awaken a child and not mold or manipulate a child's creative spirit within.

This sensitivity with our environment is something that the Christian might pay attention to. Bertrand Russell used to say, "When all is said and done, it would be a pity if mankind turned out to be no more dignified than an ape playing with matches on a petroleum dump." Indeed, now is the time either to destroy or to create, especially in a nuclear age.

Using this analogy, we are called to decide whether or not we will take care of God's Body. It may be the real test of whether we can love . . . both Spirit and Body . . . if we would love the Lord our God as Spirit, how will we also show our love for the Body?

A considerable collection of sermons fill the Barrel under the category of Life Situational Preaching covering topics such as Parables, Beatitudes, Sermon on the Mount, Prophets, The Big Ten Commandments. Another grouping is Topical Preaching such as Worship, The Lord's Prayer, Doxology, then subjects about Church and the Eucharist. There's a file for Jesus, dealing with the historical Jesus and Christology. Sermons focus on the subjects of suffering and Evil, and a series covers Pastoral Care Themes. Files exist on Death and Dying and unpacking the Book of Job. Spiritual elements were addressed such as Faith, Hope, Love, and Joy.

Then a host of sermons takes up transitions such as Beginnings and Closure in Death, for special occasions of Marriage and Funerals. Lots of sermons were directed toward various seasons like Thanksgiving, Christmas, New Year, Lent and Easter, Mother's Day, the Reformation, July 4th, plus many subjects related to Youth, Baccalaureate, Colossal Vibrations, and Retreats.

A systematic coverage was made in a category called Book-by-Book, all the way from the Synoptic Gospels through the Epistles, usually a chapter per Sunday, so that the audience was exposed to a wholistic view of Scripture. I was able to fall back on Lectionary Preaching, struggling with difficult texts and facing into the exegesis of context and its message.

Advent often guided the themes of Christmas when I dealt with Faith, Peace, Love and Joy in any sermon series. I would probably have put a different emphasis on preaching, "Spiritualizing the Ordinary" if I had read the following poem.

Slow Us Down

Slow us down, warm us up
To ponder the incarnation
Of spirit and humanity
How an unwed mother
Could immigrate homeless
In a foreign country
Impoverished and unwanted
Seeking a birth of a babe
Who later was recognized
As the prince of peace
Who introduced gentle ways
And non-violent alternatives
To the blusterers of tough talk
And passer-byers of the poor
Who care less for the least
For here in a stable was wisdom
That enlightened the character
Of a counter-cultural morality
And all the King's men, women and horses
Were put to shame by their weapons
And wasteful destructiveness
No, this was the real deal
In a shift of consciousness
That saw the "Christ-mess-tizing"
of a new birth of compassion
for all the earth and everyone
who was ever left out—Welcome!

I wrote this poem when five peacemakers were facing trial for crossing the line at a nuclear plant in Kansas City but it has a different emphasis. We look at babies and we think they are cute. The story of Christmas is "pretty and cute." However I think this poem alludes to a role in parenting. Raising future peacemakers requires projecting ahead in raising responsible adults who will make a contribution for a better world. This poem does not dribble in over-sentimentality at a manger but rather underscores a lot of love and a vision for social action. To see Jesus in this light was something I was trying to communicate in my preaching.

What I felt most alive about was a category of Prophetic Preaching. Thus I dealt with the subjects of Racism, Reconciliation, Justice, and Peace issues, already noting motivation and patience in caring for the environment. I used to fall back on a sermon, "How Long, O Lord?" a takeoff on Psalm 13.

The lingering phrase "How long" repeats itself, "How long must I bear pain in my soul and have sorrow in my heart all the day?" In some ways we will never know the trouble that someone else feels because we are so involved in our own problems. "How long must we feel the stress of oppressive debt? How long will we feel the cold of winter? How long can we put up with the speed of changes and find no time for important relationships? How long must I juggle work, play and church and find any time for my dreams? How long must I deal with problems that have few solutions? How long do I build up a mountain of fears with no answers?"

Tragedy strikes everyone. Consider the events of the family of the great preacher Martin Luther King Jr. Just a little more than a year after Martin was killed, his younger brother Alfred Daniel died in an accident at home in Atlanta. Six years later, on Sunday, June 30, 1974, Mrs. Alberta Williams King, the mother of Dr. King, was shot and killed as she sat at the organ in Ebenezer Baptist Church. Yet the elder King said at her funeral, I cannot hate any man. He went on to do many good works until 1984. They had to endure. I ask, "How long will it take to remove your mountain of fears that hold you back?"

I would suggest we need a vision such as Martin Luther King's dream, "I've been to the mountain top. And I looked over and I've seen the promised land." How does the human spirit rise above the contradictions of life and face its injustices? We recall his echo of a sermon during his Nobel Peace Prize speech; he declared, "I refuse to accept the view that humankind is so tragically bound to the starless midnight of racism and war that the bright daybreak of peace and brotherhood can never become a reality."

I submit that the biggest factor against peace is a nationalism that dims the vision for peace. MLK said this: "In a world gone mad with arms buildup, chauvinistic passions and imperialistic exploitation, the church has either endorsed these activities or remained appallingly silent." How long, O Lord, will it take to change our consciousness and remove this mountain of racism and rise beyond this scourge of nuclear death? How long O Lord will I sleep "the sleep of death" before I wake up to a new vision? How long?

"How long must I endure these sermons that are so predictable and when did it start for you?" asked Ant X, trying to be difficult and curious at the same time.

I reminisce on some of my early sermons, and they appear dusty and tedious. They have lost the spark of the moment and are not usable for any other occasion; they just take up space in the back of the Barrel. I do remember giving one sermon, after attending a debate on the Vietnam war in 1967 and returning to preach at my two country churches in Indiana, only to realize that the sermon was not well received. I had made three points that supported the idea that our nation needed to reevaluate its path in support of the current war because 1) nations operate wars out of a sense of pride, and 2) God calls for a change of heart by confessing the sin of pride, and 3) God wants us to lay down the foundation for peace by admitting that we are sorry when we are wrong. This type of thinking disturbed an Elder who objected to any more sermons about war, and to ignore his warnings would end my ministry. It wasn't a Martin Luther King Jr. moment but it raised questions about the war. That's where I was in 1967 in the midst of a great divide in this country. Needless to say, I was young and expendable, perhaps always vulnerable to the more forcible voices of the Church because I did not take serious the power of evil.

Maybe it was because I started out with a sermon on a "Case for Optimism." When I look back to this speech in 8th grade at the Optimist Club Contest, I am struck by the thought that the premise of this speech buried the truth. It was better to see the positive side of any issue or at least it seemed more comfortable, certainly more hopeful. It was the way we were taught, to keep a smile on our faces and hide any negative feelings. In the world of business the emphasis was on profits, which measure forward progress and ignore the poor and environmental degradation. The speech had to end upbeat: "Two men were behind prison bars. One saw the mud and the other the stars. It behooves us to look up and see the stars."

To be honest, we sometimes have to clean up what gem of truth might have accidentally fallen in the mud. I know in the Christian faith we want the story to end on a high note—experiencing the resurrection over the crucifixion—yet a feel-good, rosy picture hides what needs to happen to correct certain negative human and environmental abuses. For instance, some might see militarism as a positive force for protecting the nation, but others might point out the truth that we are emphasizing the military and minimizing social programs. Indeed, the military has been called the biggest purveyor of violence. The balance is in the discernment of truth. The Barrel slid shut.

Bible Cover in leather art by Bob Francis

The Book of Books

WHAT IS THE ITEM that stands apart in a Room full of insignificance? At each pause in our journey around the Room I find something notable to talk about, but what makes it note worthy? Why do some things come alive like a little ant while other things just occupy the Room? What animates each item in time and space? I don't know why I would ask such a question except to take my turn in amusing myself with a search for significance in a Room full of insignificance. If I point out its significance to me, what difference does it make to the reader, except that you have become complicit in my strange curiosity? Together we accept our inevitable fate of insignificance and accumulate our place in history for those who outlast us.

Our story lives. Our story dies. It's a mystery if it means anything to anyone else. Such are the stories in the Book of Life.

The cover of my Bible lies on top of the Barrel and is the central focus of this Room of insignificance, more than all the three computers, the open window, the radio, the love photos, all the books. It stands out. Etched by the closest of friends, a brother in the intimacy of the Word, Rev. Bob Francis caught the essence of my life through the leather design. It looks something like this.

A red chalice depicting a St. Andrew cross, the logo of the Christian Church (Disciples of Christ), is surrounded by the Tree of Life or sometimes by the Faustian Tree of Knowledge depending on the context, maybe both, showing earthy roots running down deep. The roots engrave a ridged Word that telegraphs "Kroni" when announcing the combination of Ron and Toni merging into a beginning Chi Rho symbol, meaning the Christ Spirit wedded into oneness. The frame of the cover is beautifully stitched, warmed by a swirly brown hue and greenly serendipitous leaves.

This book is the Oxford Annotated Bible as the Revised Standard Version, published in 1962 as the most accurate translation from original *koine* Greek (common language) and surpassing the King James Version of 1611 as some misguided literalists would have God speaking directly in Elizabethan English even today. I only mention this since many right-wingers see the Word of God only spoken through the KJV. My study Bible (the word "Bible" means "books") is chock full of notations, references to sermon illustrations, and interpretations.

So where do we go from here? I'm missing Ant X's steady guidance. He's probably back out in the cold hibernating with his friends and I'm sitting in this Room, flipping my mind back and forth wondering how this journey is going to end. I have to dialogue with myself as if I'm my own friend, just an ant. I know, you read about Jesus consoling us to be insignificant, to be humble, not like the Pharisees parading a false sense of themselves. Boasting. The epitome of hypocrisy. Then you read in the Bible how Jesus advises us to adopt a life of service. What if that's the real answer to life's questions? All we have to realize is that we are children of God and we'll have all the self-esteem we need. But it's also developing capacity to care, to have empathy for the hurt of others, to meet human need with our resources. What we do for others may not even be noticed, which is good because one then genuinely cares, not only personally but publicly in building justice into our institutions. It may require the ability to make good choices in the communities we belong to, i.e., to make a better world. The Bible may hold the secret, but we may not be able to see it.

I turn my eyes in the direction of the Bible and realize that up in the corner is a shelf jutting from the shelves on Quadrant II holding nine Bibles of various sizes, four journals and a couple of *Peacemaking: Day by Day* booklets. Why would I keep four journals that almost act like diaries, I wonder. But then little snippets of wisdom sneak their place onto the page. Mostly I go there when I develop writer's block and I discover self-chastisement as an avenue for motivating my body and mind. There can be a lot of space between the entries, such as now when my darkness surfaces in these paragraphs, or when I think about peace.

The final two books on Peacemaking have these Day by Day quotes, which stop you in your tracks, to make you pause in prayer as a method of demonstrating nonviolence or as meditations to remind you how horrid the thought of nuclear war would be. All roads can lead to peace at the end of the shelf.

In this book, for example, Reiner Maria Rilke has a perplexing quote: "Live the questions now. Perhaps you will then gradually, without noticing it, live along some distant day into the answer." To live into everything requires crossing both sides. The great question is how we resolve the dichotomy and see how to recognize significance when all we have is insignificance. So comes the binary issue of ones and zeroes. Out of nothing comes something, or is it only the other insignificant direction?

On February 7 in a Peacemaking booklet, Pablo Casals sidles up with action: "One's actions are a part of one's existence . . . One feels it a duty to act, and whatever comes, one does it—that's all—a very simple thing. I feel the capacity to care is the thing which gives life its deepest significance and meaning." One acts today without ulterior motives since the action is natural and right.

I think that all the obituaries and mass disasters might pause over the words of Daniel Berrigan on the March 9 entry: "The nonviolent hero often ends up dead . . . So does the American soldier, by the thousands. Death being cheap and common to the point of bathos. An interesting question remains: Who dies in a way that is a gift to history? Who makes it less inevitable that many others will die, in the same way, in even larger numbers, in the next generation?"

Any consideration of the buildup of nuclear weapons entertains evil madness to perpetuate our way of life by destroying the lives of everyone, which contradicts the sacredness of human life. It goes against the knowledge that many Generals confirm that the

Hiroshima event was unnecessary and the rush to spend another trillion dollars to modernize the weapons is foolish. Yet the madness continues.

"In the end we will end up in peace," came the final word from One who said, "Behold, I make all things new." If everything is destroyed by human accident or design, we will never have to worry if it's new, but of course it would be gone, at least to those on this planet. Elsewhere? Inexplicitly, it will be new to who "knew."

Ant X, who had quietly returned, explained how it sometimes is: "Ridiculous!"

An Ant's Fantasy

You, the reader, may be confused, but I am taking some literary license by putting myself into the world of an ant. I am now an Ant. I find humor in that. I'm unable to easily adopt the cover-up since I may not look like an ant, but for the moment I just feel that way.

During the winter when I recently left the Room, I didn't know if I was leaving an imaginary friend or a real live ant that was an audience for a writer. I always liked ants, liked watching them, liked the entertainment of observing their hard work. But in the dialogue that was set up in my head, I was always talking to the "other," even if it was merely an ant, which was congenial since I liked ants. I don't think it was much different from my Grandson adopting a pet Teddy Bear and calling him Brownie or naming his huge Monkey Mr. Monk. It's nice to have comfortable friends and in the case of an ant, many friends.

I left, squeezed under a crack in the patio door and made my way along the railing of the back deck. Soon I came across another ant, a warrior who was agitated and exchanged directions to the underground colony, touched antennae and took off. What I wasn't expecting was the unfolding of a war.

I came across the specter of warriors climbing on top of each other, creating this mound of frenzy and frantic gnashing of mandibles. They were lining up by rows in attack mode and ready to cross this wooden ravine against an enemy who defensively surrounded their Queen. The warriors were drones wearing

An Ant's Fantasy

exoskeleton armor, similar to Medieval knights of the Round Table attacking viciously and cumbersomely with swords but also with biting fury. The charge thrust the warriors into spearing assaults as they made slicing cuts into the flanks of the other side, and many that day were fallen heroes.

Ant X was attacked due to mistaken identity, which was understandable since over 12,000 other species exist in the world and Ant X's pheromones were detected with foreign disdain, meaning that he should have been instantly killed. Instead, he was escorted to the Queen for mating purposes. It was an honor to be welcomed into the private chambers of the Queen, who stored his sperm. Ant X was heavenly grateful for the rendezvous.

But another thing was happening here. Two societies were at war with each other. One side lined up, the ants flanking each other, and waited for the other side to take their positions side by side. Then upon a signal they charged each other, gang tackling certain workers. Fortunately Ant X found the society that was sticking up for the poor, the Have-nots, compared to the haughty, prideful stutters, kind of like the Tutsis over the Hutus, like every society in the world with one group dominating another, such as in Rwanda where a million were slaughtered in a hundred days, a civil war that divided the country not so much ideologically as much as by attitude—the snobby and the humble poor. The biting was ferocious from many directions by many attackers upon a single victim. The fighting seemed endless until Ant S decided on a bold move.

Ant S climbed onto a nearby birdbath and made himself a center of attention by speaking in a commanding voice, "My comrades in arms, we are not achieving anything by this fighting. I order you to stop! I order you to cease and desist from any more damage to each other."

And they did.

Both sides retreated to tunnels at opposite corners of the garden. Ant X and his group were talking amongst themselves and expressing fear that this armistice was only temporary. Ant E proposed, "We should retreat to a safe place since continuing to fight achieves nothing but collateral loss. We have nothing to prove here."

Ant W replied, "I'd rather we were all working together rather than against one another. Next time we get together let's just play football. Have you ever looked at those helmets? Ant W laughed, "They look like ant heads."

Ant E said, "Besides, it is more important that we protect our Queen. I vote that we escape by a side tunnel and find a new colony."

Ant X pleaded, "Come to my place. I know where we will be safe." He learned that Ant W was an athletic star, big and imposing, who could fend off attackers if they were followed. The small group of four slipped away from the main fighting by traveling under the deck behind the post. Ant E was a witty, wiry and winsome ant that set a fast pace ahead of the others, and stopped and waited for the stragglers. Sharing the directions and making sure that she would not stumble, Ant S escorted the Queen who also had the attention of Ant X. Precocious and engaging, Ant S knew the right thing to say for these unusual times of distress. They worked together in eusocial cooperation to form a bridge over some gaps by connecting their bodies so that the Queen could span the railing on the deck. The tiny claws on their feet gave them enough traction to maneuver into the Room.

They discovered a familiar path and climbed high to the second shelf jutting from Quadrant II, which displayed a Portrait of Queen Toni. Next to this portrait was a small gray statuette of two figures arm-in-arm like they were walking together. This became a new brooding ground. While the four companions surrounded the Queen, known as Queen Y, to protect her, it was also apparent and detected by their pheromones that they were acceptable for mating purposes. The honeypot species could handle more than just one mate, plugging the opening and eventually producing eggs and evolving larva that would grow into adult ants. It is not fully understood how they would turn out, since the variety is complex, but Queen Y produced enough eggs to create a generation each year.

An Ant's Fantasy

However, Queen Y knew she needed to leave this area to find new ground for nesting a colony. Ants S, E and W accompanied Queen Y while Ant X stayed behind in the Room.

To take a break from this fantasy and return to humanity, I plopped into the beanbag chair opposite the corner from the spotlight on Queen T. How amazing was our courtship! It started with my phone calls to several places and an answer to an exchange, "You don't know me but I would like to meet you."

"I can't this next weekend because I have to go back to my college to crown next year's Queen," Queen T said. "Why don't you write me a letter?"

It turned out to be the most important letter I ever wrote. It netted a life-long companion and many seasons of adventure.

I called Toni "Nefertiti" of Egyptian fame. My Queen Nefertiti was so beautiful, with her Parisian crown of stylish black hair, her smooth skin and her wide smile and intelligent proportioned eyes launched over a V-necked dark dress. Elegantly beautiful in her Portrait, she expressed exciting serenity that dismissed depressive moods. I was forewarned of the wrinkles of old age by checking out her mother Alice, a spunky thinker, gardener, quilter, stewardship contributor. But gazing on this Portrait of my young Toni was to see a kind, wonderful human being. I would always be in love.

I wrote to my Love in a Book of Poetry, *Five Faces of Love,* saying lovely utterances like "Never far from the music deep in my vibrations, I hear your music resonating deep in my soul."

I paused for a moment. I looked back before leaving. I felt better.

Backyard from open Window

Quadrant III

An Open Window

"Well, how's it going?"

"Pretty good. I got to spend some time with the Queen," responded Ant X.

"Is that why you look so longingly out the window? Hoping to catch sight of her?" I asked.

"I do want to see her again," said Ant X, almost pleadingly as he scanned the back yard from the sill.

"I mean I really want to see her," he spun around, losing his balance and falling onto the Ooma phone box and bouncing off the Google WiFi box located below the window. Something like a head concussion gave him a headache and a fuzzy vision of a Zen-like Yin-Yang symbol in the distance.

Sharing the vision made me wonder. The huge black and white symbol came perfectly in the best of times to describe what was occurring. The black-filled Room had toxic waste seeping in from the outside, full of cultural and political wars, but the Yin-Yang holes allowed some light to enter or let you out. The open window was an escape from this Room of darkness.

The Taoist symbol is a complementary inclusion of the opposites yin and yang. Yin is a way to think about femininity and play with some elements like softness, passivity, water, night, even death. Yang is the opposite, representing masculinity and picking up elements like hardness, activeness, fire, day and aliveness. A split in the duality creates division, even war, until the Yin-Yang returns back to balance.

I suppose this would be a way to think about insignificance and significance, depending on whether you were thinking about something negative or positive. What would be significant to some would be insignificant to others. I might have miscalculated the insignificance of people's lives in the adventures of their stories and the people who love them. There is a story to tell to the universe written on a single sheet of paper stacked on top of another to compile the history books.

The great question is how we resolve the dichotomy of opposites and know how to recognize significance when surrounded by insignificance. So comes the binary issue of ones and zeroes. Out of nothing comes something, or is it only in the other direction? The Room under the Yin principle is winding down the energy until it blacks out, although its blackness comes from outside forces setting a mood for "fast food" values. Just as some "fast food" is not healthy, so some junk politics are destructive to the common good. Ever since the 2016 election many chose junk religion and politics in preference over healthy food or any healthy alternative.

My attention was given to the Animated Shorts category in the 2018 Oscars, particularly to a little film called "Negative Space," in which the father taught his son how to pack suitcases without wasting space. He could tightly pack any container. When the father died and laid alone in his coffin, the son peered over the edge and commented, "What a waste of space!" Would anyone be that honest in an obituary to comment on the deceased's legacy, whether one really amounted to anything or told the truth about the whole scheme of things? People's fifteen seconds of fame can be short, hardly recognizable except to a few whom they helped. And in the whole range of things, who really cares except for what they themselves are going to say next? One redeeming caveat—it may matter to someone.

Ant X was poised to suggest an adventure outside but I interrupted his thinking. "So what kind of food are you eating these days?"

"The usual." Ants have storage capacity in their "social" stomach and communicate to other ants the direction and source of food by regurgitating the taste of their pheromone.

The window was there for a reason, since it represented an escape from this Room of blackness into transparency. It was a way to expand. Maybe that was one way to search for significance. Look at how something expands. Ant X chimed in at this point, "Expand what?"

"What do you suppose?"

"The economy," ventured Ant X to the poser. "Money is the driving force that makes the world go around. Absolutely. People devote their waking hours to a job for survival and support of their family."

"Even the 1% richest are never satisfied with enough," I said. "They want more and more, and the wealthy around them applaud their effort. Well . . . some work for the common good, but too often these types turn selfish in their political thinking and feel no sensitivity for the poor." I underlined the need for the future Poor People's Campaign.

"What would it take to discover significance?" I asked.

"Idealism," suggested Ant X, who pointed his left antenna to the sky, "meaning 'Swing Left.'"

"It probably would take an empathetic heart to care about those who suffer," I conjectured, not expecting much response from the indifferent. "I'm always amazed at the story of Albert Schweitzer types. He changed his career from a classical pianist to a life of service to become a physician in the heart of Africa," I said. "Significant because of highly developed skills and a belief in the peace and justice of God."

"People observe something unique about someone who sets himself or herself apart and becomes famous for one reason or another," said Ant X, gesturing to the Good Book. "Taking up the cross to follow a life of service?"

"Where do these over-achievers go?" I wondered.

Ant X responded, "I imagine that we see them as stars and they fill the holes in the cosmos with twinkly lights."

Garden corner

Garden

"I'm looking at my garden space, only six by twelve feet, surrounded by rectangular railroad ties. Purposely small, the space is manageable for five rows of lettuce, beans, zucchini, tomatoes, carrots, radishes and marigolds. I think we should go out to it," I said.

"I will take a short cut," said Ant X as he slipped under the window, out to the sill, across the east side to the railing of the deck. He proceeded down the stairwell and met up with several of his acquaintances and the author. Ant X then started in the underground tunnels, a maze of various broods, and cleared some of the larger dirt pieces using his mandibles like a caterpillar front-loader.

This spring day, following the threat from a winter frost, felt hopeful for planting a garden. I liked the sound of that. A garden itself is hopeful and connected to the organic smell of fertilizer and sweet aroma of growing vegetables. A garden lets you participate as a creator and patient provider watering the soil. One of the benefits of long-term gardening at our home is the use of imagination to name names of loved ones and sprinkle their ashes and their name tags throughout the green leafage. It's as if our friends are never far away; we produce memorials to their living presence. But the temporal conditioning of these memories implies that life is seasonal and very precious.

"Before I start to plant these seeds, I'm going to put up this roll of chicken wire once I stake the poles next to the perimeter of the railroad ties," I said to Ant X. He came peering from one of the tunnels with several of his friends.

I was rearranging name tags shaped like tiny croquet sprockets and asked Ant X, "Where are you going?"

"I have a meeting with the Poor People's Campaign. I'll tell you about it later."

"Play safe!" I looked around the garden and spotted tags instead of names of various irises—names from critical junctures in our past. For example, Larry Hake was my roommate and a motorcycle enthusiast with an arm prosthesis. Seeing his name brought to light a rambunctious memory. We acquired the Hoven House bell at Northwest Christian College and our group of pranksters decided to have a little fun by taunting the bravado of the Hovenites. I rode behind Larry on the passenger seat of the bike and shook the bell's clapper during the evening vespers, and the Hovenites angrily put up a huge food fight against us, pelting us as we circled the square at Hendrick's Hall the second time. We were strongly encouraged to return the bell the next day, actually under the threat of expulsion. That's what I shared about the brief life of Larry at his funeral following a car accident—a shy guy whose life ended without a whimper. Except I was there to note his passing, like many ants before him, small and insignificant.

I will never forget the legacy of another person honored in our garden. Alice Brooks, Toni's mother, gave us colorful life lessons from her inexhaustible knowledge of the beauty of irises and quilts, which carried over when she shared this beauty by helping to build school houses in Swaziland. I mentioned at a Memorial service that "harm to one person was harm to all gardens, to know what it means to be stewards of the little things." She walked tall in our garden.

I called after Ant X who was now followed by Ants S, E, W, plus an army of about 50 ants picking up the pheromone trail, climbing up the chunks of dirt clods and past the dirty brown blades of grass. Around the next turn they made it almost to the shed before they were attacked. This swarm of warriors, equipped with full-body protective gear, rushed full force at Ant X and company, who calmly stood their ground without raising weapons or appearing antagonistic. The warrior in charge demanded, "Who are you and what is your purpose?"

Ant X quickly responded, "My name is Ant X and I am a spokesman for the Poor People's Campaign. We are a group who represent those without a voice, those who struggle to work so that the economy might grow, those who are seeking worker justice."

This was no time to look aggressive. Neither was it a matter of indifference since the ants cared about issues, but not enough to start a war over poverty. In fact, Ant X and his company were trying to be as invisible as possible but obviously, their mere presence presented a dilemma for the bully types. Usually one can retreat with no loss of one's pride, since winning a war offers no accolade if someone is going to be hurt, especially if fatalities are involved.

Unfortunately it mattered enough to someone that someone different could not pass by even if they were almost invisible, like ants. And that's a problem, someone getting too close and making a big deal out of something as inconsequential as taking up space.

The commander declared, "You will be arrested for trespassing and causing disorderly conduct." Ant X and others were detained, issued unlikely court dates, and taken to the rustic, orange-streaked shed that contained a riding mower and a push mower. They gathered at the amphitheater for summer activity while the grass grew and the robins listened for squiggly worms beneath the ground.

Guns

I RETURNED TO THE Room and slumped into the beanbag to assess this flight of fantasy with what might be called a war on poverty and to grieve over the Parkland massacre. I was in tears in my heart over the slaughter in Florida, not that I was immune to the mass exterminations at Columbine, Sandy Hook and Las Vegas, after which weeks passed and nothing changed, as if the next excitement was anticipating another shooting. I was sick over the comments of church people who defended their right to a gun, even assault rifles in a crazily deranged and misprioritized society. When the climate turns "gun-nish," the Room turns dark for me. Upon hearing about the Florida incident, I wrote this brief letter, published by The Kansas City Star, the kind of letter that falls on deaf ears of gun-right advocates:

"Not Again in Florida on Valentine's? Only unspeakable silence can face unspeakable tragedy. But silence from Congress becomes a sin of omission. Loud advocacy for guns hurts common sense and turns unhealthy in a cultural war. Junk values hurt our society with easy availability of guns, slaughtering too many victims. What if guns have an effect that's the opposite of protection and you only gain ownership of a destructive side of life?"

This was a statement on the kind of society we really want. Now young people are speaking up. The tide is changing. The recalcitrant position of the National Rifle Association is suspect and teetering on flimsy ground. Actually, their position is set in concrete because they defend it with guns.

The NRA members hide behind the Second Amendment right, even though they suspect it emerged so that militia could be called for defense after the Revolutionary War. This amendment does not grant a right for assault weapons. Both just and unjust laws exist. The right to bear arms may not be a just human right if the universal arming of citizens promotes fear and an exaggerated loss of lives. In other words, it is fair to raise questions about the way the Second Amendment is twisted to support the use of assault weapons.

Once I said in a poem,

"Gun toters have caved into their fears, which only takes us back to wild west solutions. Then we adopted a cowardly way to handle problems, rather than finding real courage to rid violence."

Calling gun advocates "cowards" is putting lives at risk because name-calling angers the offended. However, the use of guns to protect oneself from a distance ignores more rational solutions. Maybe the willingness to face the ant-like qualities in all of us would lead us to adopt more non-violent solutions and bravely accept our mortality no matter the outcome. Trying an alternative to murder, certainly, is better than shooting someone. Does it matter if we risk our own death before our time? What does an ant know?

Mowing

THE SOUND OF DRONES is everywhere. Actually it's the sound of mowers doing the "Keeping up with the Joneses" routine of looking good in the neighborhood. For some it is the most meaningful thing they do all week. I can't stand it!

Here's what I like about mowing. It's predictable. The grass grows. It needs cutting. If you have a riding lawnmower, it appears like you are working when you really aren't. Well, maybe there's work in starting it up, but you sit there and enjoy the ride. The satisfaction in mowing is the accomplishment in making straight lines and overlapping the rows. Mostly it's sitting back with a beer and scanning the results. It's uncomplicated and requires few thinking skills.

What I don't like about mowing is the noise. During the summer one of the six neighbors cranks up his machine while I'm deep in thought. It's the manly thing to do. Ridiculous is this secret society of these hard workers! I usually go to the open window in Room-on-high to feel superior and detect the one who deserves my silent scorn. I tell myself, "This is a test to see if I can remain peaceful in the midst of noise that sounds like a chainsaw decimating a beautiful tree." I usually fail because I'm disrupted in the middle of a project, which already is interrupted by my hesitancy in the flow of words. Once I identify the culprit I turn to disparaging thoughts over how slow the mowing goes that will unkindly prolong the agony. It happens; I endure. I have negative feelings that go something like this: "Don't they care how much carbon

Mowing

dioxide is spewed in the atmosphere from small two-cylinder equipment? Why don't they pick a better time that doesn't interfere with naptime for our grandchild? Why are they so inconsiderate and act like this is the most important part of their day?" This is the part that I don't like about summer.

But I have to admit that when I open the rugged camouflaged shed with its cranky door and then push out the Brigg & Strata PowerBuilt 9.0 riding mower, I am ready to see action. I'm ready to hear my own noise. Funny thing: that's more tolerable because it's on my own terms. I console myself in saying that this insignificant evil is accomplished in a quarter of the time and at a reasonable time. So goes my running dialogue in justifying my noise climbing over my neighbor's fences.

What is it about neighbors that is so annoying? For one thing, they are indifferent. Their timing is at odds with harmonious noise reduction. Their ideology is confrontational. They are not interested in sharing the same worldview. They are the closest experiment in getting along with another when space is required. Admittedly they can be helpful when watching your property or when loss occurs. The need to mow is great small talk, and mowing is one of the significant things to do when doing insignificant things. Neighbors are great to have but probably not next door to each other. It is nice to have exceptions unless you need to be alone to write, about them.

Waterfall

"Hey, I'd like you to go with me to see the most fascinating feature of this back yard," I said, gesturing to my little friend.

Ant X followed with some tediousness, making a detour around a cauldron that served as a fire pit. A couple of park benches circled the setting used for night serenades and relaxation in viewing the fireflies in June. Ant X contemplated for a moment and opened his eyes upon a waterfall in the distance.

"How did this get here?"

"One day I got the idea for a water feature and went down the street and rented a Bobcat, a smaller front loader that started me digging a hole shaped into the letter H and piling the dirt into a mound on the backside. I shaped the rubber liner around the hole and cradled huge rocks positioned for a waterfall, highlighted with colored floodlights along the mound. The pumps were discretely placed and controlled from the house. Isn't it beautiful?"

"I bet you love to hear the sound of running water?" inquired the Ant, scratching his head with his left antenna.

"I do. It's very soothing."

"Why is that?"

"I don't know if you sense it or not, but there is a mystery attached to this place," I ventured to be provocative.

The ant stood up alertly. "What's that?"

"Well . . . when I piled the rocks along the side and channeled the water in a certain direction, I identified with the flow and began to feel a kind of Yin-Yang sensation with the water and rocks." I thoughtfully guarded my words.

"Really!" Ant X appeared skeptical.

"I can claim my own feelings. Can't I? Besides, this holds the secret to my significance," I argued.

Ant X observed philosophically, "Or . . . maybe to the ground of your non-being. It looks like death and life are played out here in the recycling of nature. I've never seen so many frogs giving birth to tadpoles and fishes abandoning small fry . . . what's with that? So many small fry after the winter we've been through."

I sat in the Gazebo relishing the moment. One of my best building projects was this structure, crafted from cedar boards and shingles. I could claim, "I built it with my own hands." I felt sufficiently bolstered by my accomplishment.

"So you built them yourself, both the waterfall and the Gazebo?" Ant X affirmed.

"That's right!

"More important, its location was enhanced by the neighbor's huge pond in which I could observe geese and a variety of wildlife fly in to mate and make temporary homes," I noted. "And the bullfrogs bellowed their presence late into the night."

"You are secluded in a refuge inside suburban civilization," Ant X observed. "Pretty lucky!"

Ant X proceeded to crawl over the railing of the Gazebo and find different vantage points to look around the yellow azalea leaves and still catch sight of the tumbling water flow. The squirrels jumped to the domed rooftop of the Gazebo, springing from nearby redbuds and playfully chasing each other across the laptop interior and disrupting the flow of the written word in rhythm with the cascading of the water flow.

The Sailboat

"Where you going now?" I asked.

"I see where you keep your sailboat," Ant X noticed.

"I store it in the backyard during the winter and have fixed it up to sail on Smithville Lake for the last 30 years," I said after viewing it from my window, knowing that just a quick glance gave me hope and restored my aliveness better than blood pressure pills.

I got into the sailboating business when I was doing leisure ministry with the Lake of the Ozarks Parish. With encouragement from my brother-in-law Dale Shetler we acquired a discarded motorboat from the old days of doing campground worship by circuit travel. We traded it in for a steel pontoon, which was a bad idea since the pontoons were so heavy. But this was a two-family project that had us sealing the pontoons, painting the sides orange and yellow, covering the top with a green canopy and mounting the corners with lollipop circular designs that were rescued from a "Strip" trash dump. It was called "The Lollipop," which you could spot from miles around. It provided hours of satisfaction for swimming and cookouts when one could find coves that would escape big cruisers, which pushed high wakes over our smaller Lollipop raft.

Eventually we traded the pontoon for a sixteen-foot O'Day sailer and had many hours of enjoyment and learning of the language and tacking of the boat. The mystery of sailing relates to Bernoulli's Principle; a vessel can tact against the wind since a faster wind directed to the outside of the sail creates a differential that moves the boat forward. I remain in awe that it works.

Even rowing the dingy from the dock to the mooring was part of the fun. Each season the preparation involved sealing cracks, polishing the surface and scraping out wasp homes. Each year the launch date was a major fixture of the summer excitement.

Sabbatical Sailboat

Sabbatical II is the second sailboat that we put on Smithville Lake in the last 30-plus years. It was like a sabbatical from the work and demands of hectic life. The other connection to its feeling of freedom was that Sabbatical II was a 21-foot San Juan boat. Several times we had vacationed on the San Juan Island in Washington and found ourselves transported to a fairyland of purple wisteria, a mysterium of art fantasy, and a harbor chorus of singing halyards. How could so much pleasure be absorbed through the years while one barely noticed any wrinkles in time?

When I survey the back yard from the window, I take a deep breath after spotting the sailboat and feel exhilarated. Soon I realize I will be moving forward once I check the wind for a 10–18 mph southern breeze and a comfortable temperature. It is not

The Sailboat

something we can plan on like a date since sailing is a spontaneous moment that requires flexibility, but when it comes together—all the forces and timing—there is rarely an exceptional moment that is more passionate. Rare indeed, like the sight of a scintillating diamond glittering off the surface of the sea.

What is it about a sailboat that immediately makes me think "freedom." It's more than escape from daily insignificance but it's forward motion against strong winds. The use of Bernouli's Principle helps understand how wind to the outside of the sail creates a vacuum that propels a boat forward, thus putting the sailor in touch with a wonder of nature and an indescribable freedom.

When I look high onto the mast and hear the luffing sails, I realize that I am most dependent upon the wind in order to move forward. When I think of Congress and the inertia of the conservative party, I feel like it is time to move in the Sabbatical by feeling the wind. Perhaps this is the way it is supposed to be. For as I rely upon the "pneuma," the wind of God, I begin to see that my recreation is really "re-creation." I also begin to notice that I can note sacred signs along the way, slow down and give permission, "Children at Play."

I adjust my cap a little, wink at Ant X and comment, "I'll have to take you sailing when the time is ripe, like a Sabbath moment, just right for all forces to unite. That's hope!"

Mac Computers

THE NEW AGE DID not wait much for slow pokes. I remember how some resisted the computers; then soon they were fascinated by the eye-hand coordination of the mouse. They took the bait and were trapped for a lifetime, merely a blip scurrying around on a window.

In 1982 I discovered one of the earliest Commodore 64s in Kansas City and started to save images for manipulating newsletters for various church and peace organizations. And then when I acquired one of the first Mac SE computers, we thought we were really something, hiking the Mac over our shoulder like a backpack and traipsing it around town to do our bidding. My friend became obsessed and mastered technical moves that compiled indexes of useful images. We were finding the Internet a source of information that had us curiously hooked.

We would find ourselves in these long-standing arguments on which was the best computer. The business model of Microsoft founded by Bill Gates provided tension for the MacIntosh imagined by Steve Jobs. The Apple side of computer development was easy to like—more friendly, more intuitive, more icons savvy. I must say, we had our elitism in favoring the Mac over PCs but it really was a lesson in how prejudice begins.

It all seems wildly irrational that I should have so many computers, each doing specific tasks and each taking up space for different reasons. When the Mac Book Air came out in 2008, we had a solid computer that could travel about anywhere, but now, of course, the smartphone transforms how people interact and behave with each other, mostly with their eyes glued to their small screens. And while I was writing this book, two out of the three devices were not working well. It happened quickly that the computers became outdated and the older programs would not mesh with the upgraded hardware. So I was having to keep up with software staying current with the hardware so the systems would operate interactively.

"When it works, it's WOW," I exclaimed, "like the name of my wife's computer, which was designed for computer-challenged old folk."

"And when it doesn't?" Ant X chimed in.

I quickly added, "It's the worst frustration I know."

"The worst."

"Yea, I want to bop it on its head!" I smacked my hands. "Some of the worst times are when I have to verify a different password or am forced to use a different user name. Totally confusing!"

"Pop!" Ant X threw his two antennae together like a laptop slamming shut.

"The other issue is that we really are not saving paper. This paperless society never materialized. We have increased the use of paper to make copies of metadata. We are complicating our lives rather than simplifying," I said, sitting back, rather satisfied with my pontification.

"You express some feelings about this," said the little ant, who had no stake in the idea.

"I think what I'm feeling is that computers seduce us into a way of life in which we are first insignificant, then we can't figure out how to solve problems, but ultimately we are dependent on computers because of the problems." I quixotically threw that new question out there.

"Okay, we are living new here and we are not even prepared for what's next," said the ant timidly.

"Wikipedia carries a great history and origin of computers, which is interesting to those fascinated by the Internet and digital flash world. Since 1984, we've had an explosion of the use of computers, and it's been fast and exciting. Who wants to go back, even though it might be frustrating and are resisting to those of us who are caught in the middle of this transition resisting something better?" I asked.

"And so we go on," said Ant X, prancing around the back side of a makeshift desk constructed out of a 4x8-foot plywood propped on a saw horse and two cabinet ends, camouflaging discarded scanners, filing boxes and spaghetti-like wires. "I could get lost in all this."

Piles of Perplexities

A‍NT X COULDN'T CONTAIN himself any longer after scaling this stack of papers. "You have a totally awful mess here."

"I don't know what you mean," I said. "It makes perfectly good sense to me."

"I'm going to call you out on that. You have piles of paper that you intend to address someday but you don't have time to read and most of the time you don't know how to make a decision about it."

I was trying to reflect on how the process usually goes. I go and pick up the mail—an increasingly heavier load. Around the end of the year I make a list of those non-profits that I want to support, particularly peace groups since I know that fewer people might support peace projects, but I also sprinkle in some environmental groups, some home colleges and justice groups. These are groups that communicate their addresses with one another and soon the requests become demanding and unmanageable. Since I already consistently support three churches each Sunday, the incoming mail is prioritized according to need and, in some cases, the mail goes directly to the recycling basket.

More significant mail might make it to the Room and find itself in one of several piles. One tray is reserved for contract papers that need a response. Another pile is almost stacked to the ceiling and contains humorous anecdotes and various forms of entertainment. A third stack is for magazines that I hope to have time to read someday. A fourth stack is a miscellaneous pile that needs to be read and determined if it needs saving. A fifth stack is a place that boggles my mind. A sixth spot is for PeaceWorks, which has this capacity to produce volumes of information that expand like atomic mushrooms.

"Why do I feel like most of these stacks would have no interest to others and as time goes on, no interest to me except for some historical perspective?" I asked.

"Because," offered Ant X, "all are inconsequential."

"Before I sift through this mess and since this is the one time I would explore this pile before I die off, and it becomes a burden for the relatives, one has to wonder why a particular item seemed important at the time," I dragged on and on as if I were searching for an item in a tax return.

"What is going on with your taxes?" Ant X asked.

"You did know, did you not, that I am a war resister? When the President expresses his fondness for jets like the Joint Strike

Piles of Perplexities

Fighter F-35—a complete boondoggle—then I think we have gone too far in military spending, at least half of the national budget, in what used to amount to 57%," I added, wondering whether we should measure our lives constructively or destructively according to how we think about our participation in the military.

I succumbed to a moment of despondency and slumped deeper into the beanbag. Notions of weapons or money drive me into these dark places. "Someone asked me, 'What is all this writing about?'"

"What did you say?" replied the Ant.

"I was hung up for an answer," I observed. "I couldn't just say that it was a book about a dialogue with an ant and how to deal with insignificance."

"Why do you say that?" asked the Ant.

"It's too silly," I chuckled.

"Maybe that's what's fun about it, how we make the insignificant so important," said the Ant.

I responded, "And we laugh at the contradictions when we make so serious the trivial things, and it's all a vain pretense that amounts to nothing."

"What do you think would be the most foolish thing I could do right now?" asked the Ant flippantly.

"That's easy. Climb that Mound of Trash," I challenged, knowing that the pile of trash gathered fifteen years of dust.

There he went. The Ant had no problem getting past the first tray but when he came to the second tray he faced a higher risk factor along the thin edge, and even more on the third tray because he needed to surmount the tightly stacked papers before figuring out how to top the loosely stacked newspapers. He was swimming in a wasteland of a recycling bin.

I watched all this from the comfort of the beanbag and requested information. "What is the headline of the paper?"

"TRUMPED on November 9, 2016, The Kansas City Star."

Then I remembered the exuberance of Donald Trump's followers. Of course, I was numbed and confused. Traumatized into silence. We were beginning a period of "ruination," a dismantling of a nation. From my perspective the voters had taken a short-sighted chance that all problems would disappear and capitalism would win the day with profits for everyone and without environmental concerns. The other issue for me was that we were impoverishing the English language, resorting to tweeting and dumbing down to the lowest common denominators of fear and sexuality. I actually said, "I'm embarrassed for our nation." Still, the happy supporters lived in dreaming innocence in a kind of carefree world of insignificance.

"What's next?" I asked, as my eyes followed the Ant jumping to the next sheet of paper. It read, "How to Stay Young," by George Carlin. The first tip was to throw out nonessential numbers, like age, weight and height. It added, let the doctor worry about them. Come to think about it, we expend a lot of energy on numbers like weight because what is unique and essential is what makes up our individuality. How we appear and what we wear absorbs our daily anxiety. "What, me worry?" What to wear is a daily concern that takes over our lives, but does it become more significant than it needs to be? Obviously, it absorbs our time if we are trying to make a good impression, but is it as significant as we believe? Or less so? Where does authenticity enter the picture?

What came next surprised me. I had forgotten that I compiled this Birthday list: "My Top Ten Birthday Wishes for Sailing into the Sunset."

1. Love peace—resist violence.
2. Stand light and right (laugh more and be honest).
3. Empathy for the Down and Out.
4. Bend the heart; deepen the mind.
5. Be real as dirt—just as authentic.
6. Frolic two by two, like passionate dragonflies.
7. Enjoy leisure, both play and contemplation.
8. Surround yourself with fewer rules, or don't sweat the small stuff, unless you are doing a project.

9. Follow MLK's dictum against militarism, racism and poverty, and add environmental degradation.
10. Follow values of Peace, Justice, Ecology, Openness, Authenticity and Love.

Ergo, be In & Out, sailing with wind and life.
Or just wear a cap and be a curmudgeon.

"So what difference does it make that these values are personal to you and insignificant to a Trump supporter?" questioned Ant X, propping an antenna under his head.

"That's a good question because one person's value is another person's anathema," I concluded.

"I mean, unpack the list. What wish is more valuable than the others?" asked the Ant.

"Well, I would say item 10 has been repeatable in many places like the GRAND PARENTING book and the search for values in GAPS. I think the emphasis on numbers one and five stand out, but actually all of them do," I thoughtfully said.

"If you look at the pile of paper, interesting ideas go nowhere, like that one about universal health care, but that would make too much sense for the self-interest group, you know what I mean?" piped up the Ant. "Next?"

"I created 'My Statement of Faith and Ministry' when I was applying for credentials with the Presbytery because I had some illusions that I would have a more secure prophetic ministry. Now, I don't think there is such a thing, unless you are retired," I replied, answering my own question. It was a good statement but seems irrelevant a number of years later.

Bunched together in a crumbled paper blob were several letters to the editor about nuclear weapons and a magazine feature about peacemakers. And some words from "El Salvador" and "The Great Mandela," by the folk trio Peter, Paul and Mary, let you harmonize and sing your heart out and put sunshine into your dreary day.

Ant X came upon a glob of paper about exercising which caught my attention for its truthfulness: "I feel like my body has gotten totally out of shape, so I got my doctor's permission to join a fitness club and start exercising. I decided to take an aerobics class for seniors. I bent, twisted, gyrated, jumped up and down, and perspired for an hour. But by the time I got my leotard on, the class was over."

"Okay," I explained, "so the above statement is an exaggeration of what really happens: I do isometrics to keep a certain tension on my biceps and abdomen area and do some minimal cardio. But I have to admit that just dressing down is all the exercising I want to do in order to avoid a super sculpted body and accept what is acceptable through the normal aging process. And it's true, just getting dressed can be the hardest part of showing up for exercise." Other senior citizens have agreed with me.

It's called "Simplifying." The Ant came across this quip that I thought funny. "Just before the funeral services, the undertaker came up to the elderly widow and asked, 'How old was your husband?' 'Ninety-eight,' she replied, 'two years older than me.' 'So you're 96,' the undertaker commented. She responded, 'Hardly worth going home, is it?'"

"So what's going on now?" I asked the Ant.

"I'm traveling around on this desk lost in discovery, finding certain gems, such as the paper, 'On Not Being Nice for the Sake of the Gospel.'"

"I'm sitting over in this beanbag chair fuming about a President who takes us to war without declaring it legally through Congress and basically taking a country down in ruination by responding to the lowest level of fear and destruction, while the rest of us are trying to be nice," I said. I clench my teeth every time I think how nice I'm supposed to be.

"And I'm a small and insignificant Ant trying to avoid the big and overpowering Bully until it is no longer possible. I like to be nice. But when injustices cross my path, when people discriminate against another and use force, I feel like someone ought to make a stand. This may mean adding a voice to the voiceless to make things right."

In Christian circles one is always cautioned that every side must be given equal weight. Really. Is that what Jesus believes? The kind will listen to all sides in certain circumstances but one must discern values that prefer love, justice, care of creation, authentic truth, and openness beyond strict literalism and rigid rules. I always hear religious leaders say that both political parties must be given equal voice, but must they be given equal preference? If one party has a bias against the poor or they exploit the underprivileged or show no compassion for the less fortunate, then every value is not equally accepted.

So I don't mind being nice up to a point. But if you are going to use force and tough talk to push your position, better think again. I'm upset that I have to live in a Trump world that draws its energy from a lower set of survival values and that the rest of us nice guys have to tolerate the backward movement until righteous indignation gets to us before we can make our move to change or impeach.

I've lived in this Room of shadows for too long by being patient with those who maintain the status quo and those who promote militarism, worker injustices, environmental degradation and the "ism" values such as racism, sexism and Republicanism of the greedy type. Of course there are nice Republicans as individuals who are neighborly, but when as a party they can create policy that turns mean and exclusive like with health care, then we have a problem. They fail to recognize the evils of institutional racism and how important it is to allow grace to lift up those who can't lift themselves up by their own bootstraps, to rise out of poverty. I wait for the light to flicker away the darkness and remove any policy that oppresses the vulnerable.

Healthy Religion

Ant X scurried around on top of the desk climbing over the printer, up and down the filing trays, and spotting one paper, "A Mainliner's Search for Spirituality."

"Whew . . . why are there so many options? Are some choices healthier than others? Who are Mainliners?" came a plethora of questions from the anthill.

"Young persons report that they are looking for a deeper spirituality, not a search for religion," I answered. "Many are zealously caught up in conservative religion that provides clear answers to a changing and confusing world. In the beginning faith development finds comfort in knowing that there are answers while mainline religion recognizes the complexity of deeper thought."

"What's an obvious difference between the religions?" asked the Ant.

"The largest Christian conservatives are Evangelicals who are in the business of conversion. They believe that faith in Jesus is a stepping-stone for salvation and a means to achieve Heaven by an act of conversion. Basically this means a public confession of faith in Jesus and several methods of baptism, a believer's baptism by immersion or infant sprinkling. It's somewhat different for Mainline churches that cooperate with one another rather than remaining independent of one another. People join a Mainline church to become Christian by working to fix the injustices and abuses of what's wrong with the world such as militarism, racism, poverty and environmental destruction, You might say they are members

HEALTHY RELIGION

of social justice churches," I said, suggesting another way of thinking about it.

Ant X interjected, "You do hear people say, 'It doesn't matter what religion you choose because we are all going to wind up in the same place anyway.'"

"I wonder."

"Is there a distinction between a healthy and sick religion?" asked the Ant.

"I think I want to say at least the following: healthy religion promotes an outreach beyond self rather than securing a place in heaven, and certainly at least this, a coping with reality rather than an escape from this world."

"Anything else?" asked the Ant.

"Well, yes," I added. "Healthy religion offers an inclusive community and can cooperate with other churches rather than going alone with a narrow set of doctrines.

"The ability to be ecumenical seems to be a factor in moving forward and growing rather than staying stuck in the past in one room with only one absolute world view."

"That's a problem, being stuck in a certain worldview," the Ant was trying to affirm.

"I know what that's like," I said, "because the Evangelical point of view seemed so airtight, since a commitment to Christ implied a timeline of the creation story and an early understanding of the New Testament church and the future design of God's plan. And to question any of it seemed to cave in the existential meaning of life."

"Where did the chink in the armor begin?" the Ant asked.

"Probably questioning how old the earth was . . . because sensible science makes the earth older than what it appears, which over a period of time melts the rigidity of false premises."

"So are you saying, in the passage of time, Bingo, the opposite point of view reveals a greater truth? You keep hearing about creation while in the back of your mind you realize you need to adjust the scientific timetable. A liberal position that allows for scientific data makes more sense than a narrow, literal interpretation that doesn't support rational thought. It takes maturity to be flexible in the faith!" concluded the Ant.

Another insight for understanding healthy religion is the way one views Jesus, not as a popular charismatic leader but as a counter-cultural force who resists oppression of the poor. Healthy religion sides with the poor, counters oppression and favors the minority position. "When following social justice concerns, I always found the following phrase useful: 'Comfort the afflicted and afflict the comfortable.' Healthy religion does that!"

Tillich Volumes

My grandfather would start his prayer for meals, "We acknowledge you as the giver of all good." If God were to be a proprietor of the good side of life, does this mean that a lot of the bad side is left out? This seems to underscore an optimistic bias for the good things of life and at the same time shuns the bad things like nuclear waste and nuclear winter.

"Isn't that a good place for religion?" pipes up Ant X, "To be positive."

"True!" I confirmed, "It's the easiest way to understand God."

"What is the hardest?"

"To come up against a verse like Isaiah 45:7, 'I form light and create darkness, I make weil and create woe,' meaning good and evil."

"What?"

"You know, God created everything. But this is where some depart from God. Two atrocities came out of WWII—the Concentration Camps and the Atomic Bomb. One turned into vicious treatment of human beings and the other turned out to be a dump of radiation waste."

"Humans are the cause, not God," chimed in the Ant X, crossing his antennae across his chest.

"There is a concept of the 8th day of creation, after which God created for seven days and on the 8th day God turned the responsibility over to humans."

"And . . ." stuttered Ant X.

"Rather than escape from the world," I reconfirmed, "healthy religion accepts its responsibility."

On the Tillichian Road

ANT X BEGAN AN arduous journey, a little erratic at first until he could find his direction west after he skirted along the edge of the desk, past the printer. He paused on the colorful protest buttons, such as "Wars are poor chisels for carving out peaceful tomorrows," by Martin Luther King Jr., and "Poetry is an act of peace. Peace goes in the making of a poet as flour goes in the making of bread," by Pablo Neruda. The buttons always seemed to widen the range of one's vision, such as "Ask not what you can do for your country; ask what you can do for your planet," or "Fight Truth Decay."

Leaving the buttons behind, the Ant crossed over to elevated shelving displaying resource books, such as a commentator's interpretation and concordances for cross-referencing certain words with scripture and verse. One shelf had the Septuagint New Testament in koine Greek, which provided a word study for making the interpretation of scripture more than just a comment on a flat, literal Bible.

My most treasured resource was the "three volumes in one" of Paul Tillich's *Systematic Theology*. I think the language of Tillich possessed a bright lightness that spoke to me about difficult, obscure subjects in the same magnitude that Paul the Apostle and writer elevated koine Greek to speak of resurrection and a rising from the dead. I was thoroughly grounded in digging through the fertile soil of Tillich's worldview, and the result was the sweat and tears of a deeper appreciation of Being.

Concerning the starting point for a theological discussion, I found it made greater sense to begin with humanity and then point to supernatural reality, or better yet to accept what we know and then raise questions. One could talk about the experience of estrangement, suffering and loneliness as an element of existential being. What it meant to be finite, feel brokenness, be vulnerable to death was to experience elements of creatureliness. But that juxtaposed another reality that was essential in giving us hope in a Spiritual Presence. Discussing the distinction between existential and essential reality became a way to talk about all kinds of things about human beings, Jesus the Christ, Church, God, the Lord's Supper, and to enjoy these amazing links of discovery in probing the mystery of the cosmos.

The parallels fit alongside each other in lining up the existential categories. The human, Jesus, the congregation of the church, the visible earth of God, the bread of the Eucharist share a notion of the body in the make-up of body and spirit. One can talk about the physical, visible, man, historical Jesus, building, God in what we see and touch, brokenness, finiteness and objects of existence.

One can equally toss into a basket the essence of things. The dynamic of the human is being, which is one's spirit. The human being is both a physical human and a spiritual being, which allows the ambiguity of both dimensions to exist at the same time. We can speak of Jesus the Christ as a physical man who points to a spiritual reality, the Christ. What if we looked at the body of God as anything we see and touch, and linked the Spirit of God as the energy that is in the cosmos? We can make further allusions to Church with a small c or large C, as a local congregation with a small c, or the Universal Church in every place and every time with a large C. Likewise, we can refer to the bread of the Eucharist as the physical body of Jesus and to the wine as the Spiritual Presence of Christ, connecting both to the crucifixion and resurrection of Jesus the Christ.

The little creature jumped up from his meditative pose on the book in question and blurted out, "Good grief! This book is as thick as the Good Book, needing another commentator."

I quickly added, "Well, you can see when I was studying it, I underlined about every other line and infused copious notes in the margins."

The Ant surmised, "You must have been confused."

"I have to admit I had to reread many sections over and over, word by word." I shook my head, exasperated.

The Ant wanted to know, "What were some of the major themes?"

"I just liked starting with the ontology, 'to be or not to be,' then to give meaning to existential being and essential being. And finally to mix all that up. I can see how that lends ambiguity to life and also separates and unites love, which Tillich defined as the drive to reunite the separated. I liked the support to my notion that one's basic core value was the drive toward significance.

"Other systems were equally valuable for pursuing social justice, such as Reinhold Niebuhr's *Nature and Destiny of Man*, Martin Luther King Jr.'s writings and sermons, and Process Theology's ability to deal with change. All these sources became my colleagues who enabled me to develop my own worldview. Paul Tillich was most persuasive, although I confess I did not understand him half the time, but I did try to entertain his ideas as other sympathetic theologians applied them. The language was hard to understand but provided a lightness of being."

Quadrant IV

Out of the Nuclear Malaise

The Trump dump has demoralized the American spirit to its lowest level. According to Maslow's hierarchy of needs, we would be sinking into greed, taking care of number one and fighting fiercely for our survival. This is not a healthy way to live, and not helpful to the next generation.

I sit on my beanbag in my little Room and talk to my little friend and wonder about the human condition. It's hard to explain the excitement that some derive from turning destructive, like a mischievous kid secretly toppling over another kid's blocks. Do you think the Trump dump trickster feels any regret for stirring up trouble or shocking people for their reaction? It's a game for seizing the center of attention and sucking the energy from the room in a power grab.

The Poor People's Campaign came along in the winter of 2018 just in the nick of time to provide an antidote for this negative downturn. Rev. Dr. William J. Barber II, president of the Repairers of the Breach, teamed up with Rev. Dr. Liz Theoharis, co-director of the Kairos Center, to send a different message, a National Call for Moral Revival. The plan was to protest in as many state capitals as possible to object to the violence of militarism, racism, poverty and environmental degradation. This picked up on Martin Luther King Jr.'s dream in 1968 to counterbalance the evils of our times 50 years later. For instance, the clarion call to be sensitive to the poor is rarely invoked in present budget battles. Most of the money goes to support the military—some 60% by many estimates.

"Do you have to take care of people's safety needs before they can risk more creative concerns with some of the higher needs?" asked the Ant, trying to undo his perplexity.

"I suppose you are asking how many changes can people handle before they shy away from any forward movement?" I wonder about the acceleration of current events in a fast-food and fast-paced world when one needs to slow down to allow the body to catch up and integrate what's really important.

"The biggest threat of any of them is nuclear annihilation," said the Ant while climbing down the tripod easel.

He noticed a placard for an ICAN presentation, which curiously was giving him some hope. ICAN stands for International Campaign to Abolish Nuclear Weapons. It is the group that enrolled 122 countries to make a commitment to abolish nuclear weapons, leading the United Nations to adopt the Treaty on the Prohibition of Nuclear Weapons. It is in a long ratification process. For ICAN's huge effort, the group won the Nobel Peace Prize in 2017.

Predictably, those who opted out of these suicidal devices were not the nuclear powers, which instead have adopted a death wish in their own addiction to power. Nuclear states continue to justify their rationale, advocating deterrence when in fact the weapons are unusable for any side to survive—both sides lose. An enormous amount of money is wasted in the belief that nations will be too scared to use them.

ICAN leaders say we can change the conversation. We can say NO to deterrence, we can say NO to nuclear weapons because they are illegal and we no longer need to wait for politicians—we can be the ones to protest.

"I'm going to make a final statement," I declared. "We don't have to know all the statistics to know nuclear weapons are dangerous. We have polluted ourselves enough with radioactivity. After all these years we haven't even found a tight container to safely store radioactive isotopes. It is immoral to endanger future generations with such lethal substances. Humanity is too vulnerable to play around with radioactivity that doesn't easily go away.

I've listened to science and heard the plea of PeaceWorks member Ann Suellentrop with Physicians for Social Responsibility, to learn that Plutonium isotopes have different half-lives, the time it takes to lose half their radioactivity. The U.S. Nuclear Regulatory Commission says the isotope PU-238 has a half-life of 24,100 years and PU-241 has a half-life of 14.4 years. These are long destructive time periods.

"The only option is to abolish these weapons altogether," the Ant said, looking at me sadly. "Still, people want to hold onto nuclear weapons."

"The power of destruction becomes too much," I said.

"Too much, probably even if we could reach all the goals and measurements for survival of the planet, according to 350.org, including reducing our emissions of carbon dioxide," Ant X said, sweeping his antenna across his thorax.

"Enough peace groups might keep us surviving, which is the shadow to all this destruction."

Ant X went on, "Weapons of war are Unaffordable and Unusable."

"You got that from a protest sign," I echoed, "and it's true. Realizing this, we see little signs of hope in the midst of so much destruction."

The Ant sighed, "Holy creepers."

Coveting Drones

Ron and Toni before Drone replica at Whiteman AFB

ANT X HEARD THEM at first, a kind of whiny, menacing sound that was meant to keep everyone off-balanced and strike a swarmy fear of an ambush that would squeeze the victim tighter than a boa constrictor. Could it be that they were like a 666 apocalyptic assault that signaled the end, implying no escape, no hope, no breath? Sometimes this gang fly-over is a curse that brands an ant like himself with a pheromone, marking an ant as a foreigner that needs to be killed. Other times an ant like himself is marked by a mating pheromone that gives him the privilege of being carried to the Queen. Earlier, Ant X was chosen for the latter purpose. But it meant that he would occasionally leave the Room to care for the Queen in a place designated near the garden.

The Ant decided to inform his friend, "I'm going to need to take off for awhile to see my Queen."

"Will you be back?" I asked.

"I'm not going to leave you alone," the Ant was heard to say.

The military-industrial complex was manufacturing a popular but different kind of drone that could sneak up on the enemy. Drones were pilotless aircraft that were described as computer operated, accurately targeting terrorists some distance away. Drones called "Predators" and the heavier armed "Reapers" were becoming the preferred weapons.

A cloud of secrecy surrounded these weapons of choice—the public was told that these were precision weapons. Other reports came in later, but in the early years the killer drones registered a 98% failure rate. They double-tapped the victims, hitting the rescuers after the first hit. These dots on the screen, referred to by operators as "bug splat," frequently turned out to be innocent children. When you hear about weddings that are attacked by drones, you experience a negative feeling about these seductive protectors of our national defense. Drones remain in the dark shadows, hidden in a code of secrecy that sometimes only comes to light during protest marches, of which involved me personally and sacrificially.

The Midwest Trifecta Resista protests occurred during the weekend of April 13–15, 2012. The Action Committee of Peace-Works planned three events in three locations in three days, riding to Fort Leavenworth in Kansas to protest Chelsea Manning's imprisonment; to Kansas City, Missouri, to call for a world free from nuclear weapons, and to Whiteman Air Force Base near Knob Noster, Missouri, to oppose drones. Several actions ended in arrests for civil resistance.

Near Whiteman AFB, over 70 miles from Kansas City, we took a lunch break in a state park the indictment I used the microphone to read information about Drones and talk about our action on April 15. A bonding took place that helped the participants concentrate on the commitment that would be required to cross the line. Part of our preparation was a lunch break in a nearby state park and we discussed the indictment to be delivered to President Barack Obama, Secretary of Defense Leon Panetta and Whiteman AFB's Brigadier General Scott Vander Hamm and drone crews in such training places as Creech Air Force Base in Nevada for "extrajudicial target killings" by Reaper drones.

Protesters at Whiteman AFB are kept at a distance by a demarcation line at the gateway and a grassy knoll located to the left. We released black balloons memorializing the 175 children killed by US drones in Pakistan since 2008 and before 2012. The protesters flew kites for peace on earth and in the sky. The following protesters delivered statements before their arrest: myself, Mark Kenney of Omaha, Nebraska and Brian Terrell of Maloy, Iowa. Slowly we walked to the entrance while the community of peacemakers followed.

Officers came to meet us. Terrell told an officer, "We want to go to the commander" to present the indictment, to which the officer replied, "We can't allow you to do that." Terrell answered, "Our conscience won't allow us not to." We were handcuffed and escorted next to a column of the entrance adjacent to a military bus.

Busting out of the bus, some 50 storm troopers or more dressed in riot gear lined up three rows deep and proceeded by strict command marching to intimidate the other protestors. The troopers moved methodically across the entry road, sometimes pounding their chests and helmets with their batons in a precision drill. They appeared as frightening as the exoskeletons of warrior ants, and that's what this was about—a rehearsal in scaring people.

We three arrestees were processed in a building like a gymnasium. We were transported by bus to be directed to benches, and were each assigned an attendant, smartly dressed and supervised to check all property on our person. It was a sobering and humorless procedure in which we awaited the paperwork, still being authorized through proper channels. We were charged with trespassing on a federal facility and assigned a court date of June 6 to make our pleas. We were assisted onto a bus, transported to the entrance way and unceremoniously set free on the roadside to find our vehicles.

The second phase of this arrest was to answer to the charge that Mark, Brian and I "did enter a military installation for a purpose prohibited by law." When we arrived at the scene of the US District Courthouse in Jefferson City, Missouri, we entered a modern day facility built of granite, marble and glass in contrast to the former Missouri State Penitentiary across the street, which was dilapidated with fallen stone and open sores in its proud fortress of hard-knock punishment of the good golden days. When walking across the floor of the rotunda over an emblem of the state seal, one walks across an eagle grasping arrows in one talon and an olive branch in the other, surrounded by the famous justice quote from Amos, "Let Justice Flow Like a River," somewhat changed from the words "ever-flowing stream." The new courthouse was impressive. But the flow of justice was as sluggish as the nearby Missouri River and adhered to the rigidity of the law rather than the spirit of compassion.

Later Brian Terrell would submit his recall of these events in the June-July 2012 PeaceWorks Newsletter: "Our polite request (the indictment about lack of due process and killing of innocent civilians) was denied and our 30 or so companions were chased off the property by about 50 Air Force personnel in full riot gear. They performed a carefully if grotesquely choreographed drill routine, complete with goosesteps and synchronized grunts and beating of clubs on shields. Reminiscent of a Monte Python sketch or of the 'Springtime for Hitler' dance number in the Mel Brooks musical 'Producers,' this performance reveals a government literally scared silly by its own citizens."

Mark Kenney decided to plead guilty and Brian and I entered pleas of "not guilty." Mark asked to be sentenced as soon as possible and Judge Matt J. Whitworth questioned if he wanted to give up a full trial. He did since he felt that the trial was pretty much predetermined, similar to trials of many "terrorists" who were imprisoned without due process of law, without a fair trial. After another five hours the probation office prepared a presentence report and Mark was handed down a four-month jail sentence that began on July 18. The Judge advised Mark to stay out of trouble. Brian Terrell further writes, "Judge Whitworth should be informed that Mark's good Lord bids him not to stay on the sidelines avoiding inconvenience and suffering."

Brian and I pled "not guilty" and received a September trial date. Brian represented himself and I found the counsel of Ruth O'Neill, Attorney and Catholic Worker from Columbia, Missouri. We would receive assistance from Henry Stoever, who also was awaiting trial on Aug. 17 for resistance in the second segment of the Trifecta Resista at the nuclear weapons plant.

The trial gained momentum. The "drone trial" supporters raised funds for expert witnesses such as former US Attorney General Ramsey Clark, Col. Ann Wright, Kathy Kelly and Bill Quigley. This was a federal case with more at stake while many other trials have reduced penalties on the order of trespassing charges. That's why the consequences at the federal level are more severe.

The trial took place on September 10 and the gathered community responded to the media and shared poetry and dance. The front of the courthouse dipped down into a slope of green lawn and a lazy river which made a beautiful backdrop for a modern dance by Tuesday Faust, gracefully sanctifying the inner proceedings.

The details of the arrest provided some missing pieces in the recall of the officers but seemed not to discredit their account. Questions about the military theatre showed the procedure to be "over the top" but the use of drones was not questioned. Terrell did a commendable job in keeping the prosecution alert. Likewise O'Neill supported the inquiry into my testimony and statement of purpose. The expert witnesses raised serious questions about the legality of the drones and the need for civil resistance.

The sentencing phase finally came like a hammer to the slammer. I got five years of probation and Brian got six months of jail time. Eventually my probation was reduced to one year, although reporting to the probation officer was a restrictive inconvenience especially when we needed to go out of town.

It would be easy to curl up in a corner and ignore the endless wars. When someone dies miles away from us, why should we feel the grief of family members of another nationality? Why care about anything? Does it matter?

This trial was a major stand-up moment for being a human being. I had to face my fears and test my courage. I had to balance my concern for my family and try not to cause them harm. The problem with being a caring individual is the stress of seeing the injustices around us. Precisely the problem! But you know what? It would be easier to be addicted to entertainment or alcohol or a number of numbing devices, but I prefer to feel some rage over the pain of injustices.

I guess it's the capacity to feel something, any abuse, to feel righteous indignation against wrongs. One has to go through some darkness to handle the unpleasant, to tolerate some lower-level cruelty. One has to face contradictions when the light dims. During this trial, I wrote the following poem.

Edge of Darkness

    It just keeps getting shoved to the edge
    Into a shadow of darkness
    Away from the light of peace
    Relegated to the corners of the banks
    Depositing security like nuclear weapons
    Defense systems and drones
    Hovering like blackbirds
    Ready to pounce on your back
    When you are not looking.
    A small remnant of courageous idealists
    Found unacceptable the notion
    That the public good was dismissed

From devices that could trigger their death
Since the corporate powers hid
Behind closed and deceptive doors
To shut out the sliver of light
And barricade access to their private plotting.
But the single candle of conscience will flicker
Over the edge of darkness
Which at times seems pitch black
Although still the candle burns deep within
And to look up
You see more stars in the sky.

I breathed deeply, telling Ant X, "I don't know what to say. I participated in all this. Glad I did. I came alive to say that some things are wrong but maybe not the way the right wing perceives it."

"The light flickers off," said the Ant, blinking. "And we cannot see our own blindness."

"Especially if we are ignorant to the opposite perspective and not listening," I said.

Ant X made his way from the third shelf that had a special place for Paul Tillich's *Three Volumes of Systematic Theology* and Abraham Heschel's *Man Is Not Alone* and *God in Search of Man* to the fourth shelf, inch by inch, slowly gripping the sidewall with his clawed feet, when he spotted it. A huge poster board shouted out, "STAND UP KC to end POVERTY WAGES."

The Poor People's Campaign

Civil Disobedience in Jeff City

FILLING THE WALL SPACE above the Stand Up KC poster was a picture elegantly framed in velvet and black exterior surrounding a leather etching of a prophet created by the artisan Robert Francis. This beautiful gift to me at the time of his departure to Oregon symbolizes how life goes on and is remembered in our hearts. I believe it depicts Abraham Heschel, reminding me of the many times Bob and I sat in rhapsody to pore over the melody of his words.

Back to the poster "Stand Up KC." This movement in Kansas City promotes a raise for workers on minimum wage, often working in the fast-food industry. It is at first alarming to compare what they make and what the CEO owners make who claim they need that kind of money to make a profit. Soon the workers realize that these unfair conditions are wrong and they are willing to be arrested to correct the injustice. Michael Enriquez has given wonderful leadership to this unionizing effort as he has also turned his attention to the Poor People's Campaign (PPC).

Fifty years ago, before Martin Luther King Jr. was shot down in 1968, he started this effort to address the issue of poverty. He used the energy of the Sanitation Workers for marching on civil rights. Stand Up KC is the local answer for continuing the dream he started.

The national Poor People's Campaign is under the leadership of co-chairs Rev. Dr. William Barber and Dr. Liz Theoharis. Rev. Barber is a Disciples of Christ Minister in North Carolina leading protests on the legislature for Moral Mondays. This effort has been called a Moral Revival of American Values. The local kickoff against poverty happened on May 14, 2018, when about 250 people gathered at 5:30 am to march to the mural of MLK at Linwood and Troost to sing and announce plans to go to Jefferson City as others across the country were gathering at 40 state capitols. Our caravan to the state capitol ended up on Monroe, then we marched to Capitol Ave. displaying signs of "Stand Up for America—End Poverty." We crossed the capitol lawn to hear some excellent speeches. We did a "sit-down" on the street facing Capitol Avenue but were unsuccessful being arrested there, perhaps because it wouldn't be good PR for the authorities to arrest us in front of the Capitol building. So we proceeded down Main to McCarthy to do a sit-down near Hwy. 63.

The songs, resolutely vigorous, caught the significance of the moment. Finally the police discerned our resolve and set up a procedure by which they ushered us protesters row by row to a shaded park and processed us by taking our ID and filling out information for a ticket that ended up in a lawyer's basket for negotiation with ordinance authorities. One of the unique features was to identify a personality such as Gandhi or Chavez or one of the protestors by name and chant back to "Where are they?" by singing. "He would be with us," or "He is not here but would be here." This was a clever way to show the kind of people we sided up with in the face of trumped-up charges.

The arrests did not seem normal since we were not taken to a holding cell but we fulfilled the conditions of an arrest in that we did not obey civil orders. Many could not be there from St. Louis and other locations but that day, for the kickoff of the campaign, 88 were arrested.

Does it matter how many were arrested? Not really, but enough to be noted as an incident that matters. People ignore protests on poverty, on racism, on militarism, on the environment so that they can go about their insignificant lives without being inconvenienced or having to make an uncomfortable sacrifice. They may provide lip service to these issues and approve of someone else standing in for them as long as they are not put out of time and money.

Ant X interjected a question. "So why are you showing up for these protests?"

I spoke up, "I think it's the most important response I can make now, and any other time might be too late."

"What do you mean?" The Ant bobbled up both antennae in wonderment.

I became serious, saying, "There is a black hole in Washington, DC, that could lead to war with North Korea, and this might be the only chance to resist the recklessness of hostile policies that could lead to chaotic destruction."

"But nothing has happened so far," the Ant noted.

I said, "I don't know how but we have really been truly lucky—probably we can't count on this karma forever. We need more caring people to step up.

"And obviously we are vulnerable. The electorate couldn't discern the lies behind the rhetoric, and people will follow authoritarian directions without considering the consequences because they don't think ahead, or they don't care."

"What do you mean, they don't care?" countered the Ant.

"They don't seem to grow up with enough empathy to feel the pain of another," I said, leaning back in my swivel chair in the center of the Room, "but they follow the rules OK. They hurt people by their policies such as with health care and think nothing about the consequences of what they are saying."

"Mystifying?"

"And problematic."

On May 29, the day to protest militarism, I stood in front of the capitol in Jefferson City and read my poem:

The Horrors of Militarism

In 1945 we yearned to seduce Pandora's Box
And unveil the dark secrets of the atom
Hence a Big Boy bomb dropped a dilemma
Upon humanity by introducing the Atomic Age
That could show a road to total destruction
And sell a nation's soul to militarism
Into the shallow pursuit of money.

Sometimes we are drawn to the dark side
And we are lost in the red-light district of U-235
Where we discover the uranium of radioactivity
That is dangerous to vulnerable humans
Since we have no place to store it
Yet our technology just makes more
Creating an even bigger dilemma

Our hope lies in abolishing all nuclear weapons
Since they are unaffordable and unusable
As technology has outstripped moral restraint
We are good at building a stockpile of weapons
But we are only threatening our future
With a one-night stand flirting with death.

The Prophet art by Bob Francis

Real Significance

ANT X WAS STEPPING along the edge of the fourth shelf when he slipped and fell. Fortunately the floor was carpeted and he ended up in a soft landing. He stood up, brushed his eyes, and decided to head for the leisure bookshelf. He noticed the box with newspaper clippings of social action reports and the supply of printed announcements of various projects, past the scrap paper for jotting down new "To Do" notes. After he came to the corner of the leisure bookshelf, he looked up to see a ballpark hat hung on the shelf corner in memory of my father, which had the insignia "U of O" with some Oregon buttons pinned to the bright green material.

A father plays a role in how one deals with authority figures. My father was the eldest of three boys born into a prestigious doctor's family. But as nearly as I can tell my father was put down by over-controlling parents. He was emotionally handicapped in his ability to function in the world, although he managed to graduate from college and function as a switchman for Southern Pacific Railroad. He seemed to be well liked, was greeted on the street as "Doc," and was welcomed in the bowling league and as a member of the Elks. What I appreciated about him were the many games of Cribbage he played with me and he had a daily curiosity about Crossword puzzles. I underestimated his influence since I perceived a lack of higher ambitions in him but now understand more about the aging process. I am grateful that he was not the strict father of boot-camp parenting who demands obedience to a lot of rules and cultivates right-or-wrong rigidity.

Real Significance

I've come around more to accepting my father's limitations. I wanted to be proud of my Dad. Maybe I wanted him to be proud of me but was waiting for validation. Perhaps he wanted that, too, and it never came. Sad how our trivial lives are lived out. It was a wonderful feeling the day when I didn't have to prove myself to anyone else, not even me.

One of the growth spurts is to have confidence in one's job without an over-controlling personality. In addition it's great when one removes traits of perfection to make it easier for others to tolerate our quirkiness. Anyway, life is more forgiving when we can come to terms with our parents' inadequacies and love them for the gifts they give us. However, I was traumatized by poverty and shyness. I desired more confidence when I was young, and I wish I could have felt at ease around people I admired. I did feel that I developed sensitivity for those less privileged. I sometimes think that my grandchildren are doing a better job than me, but I would want them to see through the pretense and hypocrisy of false authority. I wouldn't care if they caught the protesting urge when it is appropriate.

What was charming about the Royal Wedding on May 19, 2018, between Prince Harry and Meghan was that an institution of white privilege was turned into an exercise of democracy with the inclusion of African Americans and the blurring of cultural status. I think the fascination with royalty stems from the search for significance; being seen around pomp and circumstance makes you feel better than who you really are. Which raises a question: does significance come through acquired status and wealth? On the other hand, does insignificance come from an acceptance of one's role in a democracy as one of the people?

"I am a worker drone, nothing more," said the Ant.

"To me you are so much more," I offered this as well, "when you share your love."

Oftentimes persons show up on TV or a picture is taken of them or they appear on film, having not accomplished more than that. Just showing up, and they are considered famous. They are perceived as famous, which may bring them some fortune, but fame may be from a bit of luck and a camera. It may not test their real significance of character. That would require them to share the core values that are at the heart of their well-being.

Another way that a person enhances their significance is by an old theatrical trick, "presence." What I mean by this is the focusing of energy into a stage presence that can put excitement into the performance. When the director calls for "energy," he or she is calling for something extra in the words or action to uplift the script to another level of aliveness. This instruction can lift the ordinary into a special significance.

Nevertheless, for most of the time, life is pretty ordinary. Only on special occasions, like a Royal Wedding, can one be lifted to princess-like recognition. There is a synergy that can come to certain communities.

The Ant burst into the thought process. "Are you trying to say something important here?"

"Yeah, I think so."

"How so?"

Whenever I attend live theatre I come into contact with something that enlivens me. Presence is a good word, but it could also be enlightenment, orgasm, delight, a boost in motivation, any number of verbs that offer a spirited resource. When the harmony of mind and body feels like the stresses of fragmentation are left behind, then we are in touch with a deeper energy.

I see it in the look of a fresh face that springs alive with energy. I experience it in play where one acts spontaneous and exuberantly alive to one's true self. I find it in the protest of injustice when one is arrested for standing up for the side of good. I discover it in being authentic and honest. It is stunning in appreciating the face of beauty. It is found in leisure. It is found in re-creation. It is encapsulated in the phrase: "Live into the presence."

Presence came at the right time in the form of the Poor People's Campaign (PPC). It offered an antidote to the right-wing thinking that wanted to use force to turn back every progressive idea that was trying to confront militarism, racism, poverty and environmental degradation.

Real Significance

When I was recruiting for PPC, people would give lip service to it but they were obviously uncomfortable with the idea of arrest. Here was a chance to do something significant with their life, yet they leaned toward the comfortable and safe non-confronting approach. They would choose insignificance over significance, which meant thinking up an excuse that was usually a familiar activity that was repeatable, effortless and comfortable fiddling around the house. They seemed to approve a tiny obituary in the end and an exit that would cause no one any problems.

We are taught to be compliant, but the case can be made for even shy people that there are times when we must stand up and fight back. Empires come and go but we have been under siege by the heavy-handed approach of the bully proprietors.

What haunts me about this book is the same answer that came to Jesus, saying, "Whoever loses his life for my sake will gain it."

"It seems opposite of what you would expect," Ant X boldly exclaims. "Jesus asserts an attitude of insignificance as a significant place to be."

And that realization is a wake-up call that has pushed me into a beanbag chair and now this book.

The Value of Leisure

ANT X AND I are moving to the bookshelf that has numerous books on leisure. For a good part of my career, I wanted to build a theology of leisure and engage in leisure ministry. I pursued these goals when I wrote a doctorate thesis, "Leisure Ministry: A Study of the Lake of the Ozarks Parish and Its Impact on the Local Church."

I felt like I earned the degree with hard work and a creative effort when most of the time I saw others developing routine, insignificant proposals that were not worth the time put into them. I don't know what made me think that my project should make a contribution. Maybe that was a statement about life and the worthwhileness of being placed here on earth. I felt the same way about retirement, that one should enjoy life but at the same time give something back for borrowing our time here in the moment.

I defined leisure as the freedom to concentrate on an activity that provides play and spiritual enrichment. Leisure was perceived actively as play or passively as meditation. I would go on to define the problem like this: We worship our work, work at our play and play down our worship. (I concede a small point in playing down worship instead of playing at worship—a minor point.) It didn't take long to realize that work addiction fed into our survival needs and replaced our contemplative time to gain a perspective on life. Life is "go-go-go," play hard and ignore the core values of peace and justice. One needs to assess the balance of work, play and worship to prioritize what is significant about life to discover what would give it deeper meaning. A depth check if you will, to measure what it is that might pull us up from a kind of shallow existence, asking, "How do we want to spend our leisure time?"

But if leisure is spent doing nothing with our friends and scampering about for entertainment, it may seem to be insignificant even though it's kind of like spending time watching "Seinfeld," a show about nothing. Sometimes my best ideas come after doing nothing, a whole lot of domestic chores before I can write. Our choices are often insignificant, impulses of the moment, rather than activity that would benefit anyone. Let's face it, our ultimate concerns, using Paul Tillich's phrase, have no benefit to anyone else. We languish in the enjoyment of a few friends and contribute a portion of our memories to our grandchildren. Then we die, signifying insignificance except to our friends, who will mourn for a while and recall our presence in the birth of creative thinking.

We will engage in deep thinking, relishing clusters of friends, seminars and biographies to determine our purpose in the whole scheme of the human enterprise until we finally give up. We may be comforted for a while by the thought that we are children of God, placed here to love and destined for Heaven. We may like the idea that we are here to make our contribution and we will either add a plus or minus to the human enterprise. I used to run workshops, or playshops, on "Coping With Leisure," but the work ethic was so strong that few saw church as a leisure experience. We may only see ourselves like ants, constantly busy but fulfilling our role in society, dying strong when it's time like millions before us in the cycle of life. We find it significant to ponder these things in a gazebo, observing the sights and sounds of nature. And if we know of others whose lives are cut short, as many are, then we only add to the mystery of our deep thinking.

Ant X looked up at the bookshelf as if it were a holy mountain, a symbol of high aspirations and site of great commandments. I think there is a reason that the screensaver on my computer shows a beautiful mountain. Mountains are traditionally the places where covenants are made, the law is given and sacrifices are performed. I've climbed some challenging mountains in my lifetime, but sometimes I've met my limits, such as the time I had electricity arc out of the bottom of my shoes while trying to get a youth group to a safe place for Communion.

I lay silent in my beanbag while watching the Ant slowly climb, gripping the side panel and achieving the fourth shelf, where wonderful books revealed the wisdom of leisure.

I said to the Ant, "You've crossed some wide gaps by yourself."

"Usually I find others who can use their bodies to create a bridge to span the gaps," said the Ant in a stretching exercise. "But not this time since I'm just here with you upon this mountain of higher thinking."

The mountain was a metaphor for Martin Luther King, who spoke before his death of doing God's will and looking over the mountain into the Promised Land. He said he was not fearing anything. He reached "a certain level of calmness." A readiness for death may be this "letting go" and not fearing the unknown.

It should be noted that the top shelf held a slide projector of our trip through the Mediterranean area, when Toni and I were young, before kids. We never want to review those slides although at one time we traveled from church to church putting on programs about the Holy Land. Some people have strange reactions as if they receive special powers by touching sacred sites like the tourists filling bottles at the river Jordan. The people who do this literally hold onto a fact faith rather than a metaphorical storytelling that nurtures Biblical interpretation and deep thinking. The latter approach is so much more fun and catches the spirit of the unknown, which is the value of faith. We're glad we went, but we do not need to go again.

I don't know if there is any one book on this shelf that stands out from the rest. My own journey in writing and affinity to poetry satisfies my longing for books, and now that I am getting older, I desire to lighten the load. No question about it, books are sacred pauses that give reverence to life but it takes a lot of reading to gain the wisdom of the ages. I guess now we have the wisdom of the Internet, but it is difficult to replace the intuitive wisdom that agitates deep within. That's where the protest erupts to spew over the shallow hypocrisy of evil, as in the case of the Poor People's

THE VALUE OF LEISURE

Campaign, going up against militarism, racism, materialism and ecological destruction.

"Even after reading all these books, the future is dim," I sadly said. "I intensely blame the GOP for not doing much to change the trajectory over the cliff."

"But Trump helped lower the hierarchical status so that we are one nation among many nations," lectured Ant X. "We are gifted in some areas, but not to the extent of acting superior in all areas."

"Then we can start listening and cooperating with other nations."

"We came down. Others went up." Ant X said, "Some believe that there were seismic shifts in diplomacy."

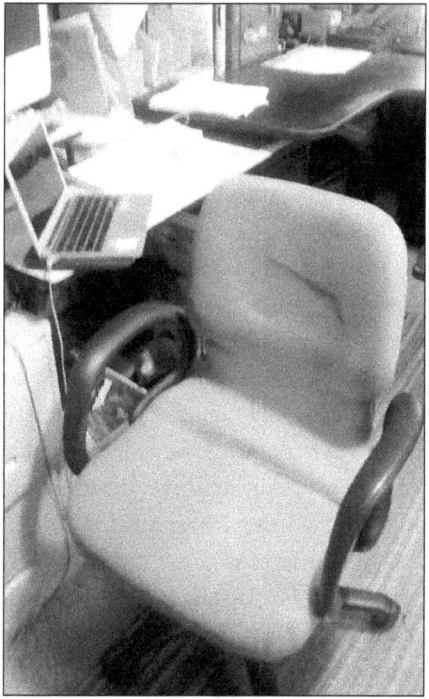

Writing Zone

The way I remembered and tried to fix what was happening occurred in the following way:

Setup for Exercise in the Room

I sit down on the swivel chair in the center of the Room. I start to spin and soon I'm out of control with images flying off the outer edges of concentric circles. I see a movie in my head where I say, "If voters elect Trump he will take down a democratic nation—he dismantles everything." Then on July 16, 2018 he turns the world as we know it upside down—allies and foes trade places, where the old order is one big "lie" and the new order is another big "lie," equalizing nation alongside nation in this eye of a political hurricane seeing new images spinning round us. Sadly, too many strong-armed leaders force themselves into control, yet meditators are one solution to counter this over-control.

> Ant X breathes in, love. I exhale, peace.
> Ant X breathes in, authenticity. I exhale, justice.
> Ant X breathes in, openness. I exhale, creativity.

This elicits a Yoga ending, Namaste. (The light in you greets the light in me.) We become still, hidden in the shadows. Then life flows on insignificantly.

Resuming reality (might you accept as much as you can believe), the Ant was going straight toward a book that had an impact on my reflection about leisure, a rather simple but profound book by Gordon Dahl called *Work, Play, and Worship in a Leisure-Oriented Society*. He talks about the distortion of these components when we make work our idolatry, play so much like work and minimize worship as insignificant. But then worship becomes significant in another book entitled, *The Other Side of Silence: A Guide to Christian Meditation*, by Morton T. Kelsey. There is a story about the fear of being alone, about becoming busy being with others, and then raising the question that if you fear being alone, just think what you inflict on others. One thing I learned was the value of being alone and having "Thinking Time." Another discovery was the book *Chop Wood Carry Water* by Joshua Medcalf. Reading this book opened me up to a lot of sexual and spontaneous serendipities.

The Value of Leisure

"I really did stockpile books on leisure and felt like the future of creativity was to give people a guaranteed income," I said.

"What happened?" The Ant looked perplexed.

"Corporations took over and forced low-wage workers into slave labor—the way I looked at it," I reflected.

"You never saw the leisure revolution in the '60s and only returned to the hard work of ant societies in the '70s," noted Ant X.

"Well, I think there is another book to write here but maybe not in my lifetime," I shrugged, feeling that it was easier to let go of some things during certain stages of life.

"I see where you have an entire shelf of Edward Hays' books," gestured the Ant, pointing to the fourth shelf.

I said, "If I were to read something I could be interested in that, but I rarely reread material or for that matter re-see movies or repeat much of anything."

"Why's that?" asked the Ant.

"I'm ready to move on. There might be something new!" I said.

"I guess you won't repeat your death," the Ant chuckled.

"Once is enough," I laughed.

Layers of Peacemaking

Picture at entrance

I SLUMP IN THE corner beanbag trying to sort out the shenanigans of the Trump train wreck and it just seems like one chaotic thing after another. I turn on the overhead lamp to read and my eyes are taken upward to a placard featuring a letterhead with a white frame showing its age, plus signs of scotch tape. The Ant immediately begins climbing to get a better look and soon realized that it is a letter from the Department of the Air Force at Whiteman Air Force Base in Missouri.

The letter reads, "On this date you entered the Whiteman Air Force Base Complex without authority. Your conduct has evidenced a total disregard for the law . . . and will not be tolerated. You are hereby notified that, effective upon your receipt of this letter, you are ordered not to reenter or be found within the confines of the United States Military Reservation at Whiteman Air Force Base, Missouri."

The next sentence starts out, "Should any compelling reasons exist which you believe would be sufficient to justify modification or termination of this order," do such and such, other than detainment. Well, what compelling reason would prompt one to come up against authority like that, other than trying to prevent a crime?

Actually I was proud of this letter and displayed it in a prominent place in the Room. It was dated August 9, 1990, after a three-day walk from Kansas City to the AFB near Knob Noster as a commemoration of Hiroshima. In the margin were the words: "My first Civil Disobedience action as a rite of passage in the peace movement on the Annual Peace Walk in celebration of 45 years of Hiroshima—Nagasaki to prevent this from ever happening again."

I struggled with this at the time because basically I was a good student and followed directions. I was quiet and had no reason to be a troublemaker, until now. Patriotism is a false loyalty when we are supporting deadly weapons that kill others unnecessarily. Now the weapons are so much more powerful, a thousand times the killing power of Hiroshima, easily capable of destroying the world. The only solution is to abolish them if we want our grandchildren to live. I don't think that is such a platitude after a closer examination of this issue. The weapons are unusable. And we are exhausting an economy no matter how much money we think we have while we are maintaining a standoff of scaring the other side, sometimes hanging onto the MAD threat of Mutually Assured Destruction, but in the end this thinking turns out to be unaffordable. Unusable and unaffordable, says my peace sign about Weapons of War.

I struggled with this for another reason. I could no longer live my life silently even though I wished to be non-violent yet stand up against injustice. What would it take to be uncomfortable enough and sacrifice money and time to be a person of principle? Anymore, people are herded around, so easily persuaded by the political forces that they are mushy and compliant to authoritarianism. They may live a long time, but are they living significantly? That is a question that we have been asking, and how much do we care?

Above our pond I love to watch dragonflies, hooked together, flitting here and there, expressing the urgency of the moment—just a few fragile weeks to live and propagate before they die, so I was told. The liberal agenda makes so much more sense in moving forward to help people rather than ignoring their needs. Seeing through the shadows, we need urgency like a dragonfly to move this nation forward on the light of peace rather than the darkness of war.

After a flood of western light splashes across the waterfall and freshly cut grass to create a maze of mysterious shadows that quiet the evening day, we can rest in peace, surrounded by greenly trees and melodious birds. The wonder of this world nurtures the soul and we find significance in majestic beauty. When the day is done, we can close our eyes and not worry about a thing since the waterfall will keep on flowing. Nevertheless, those who identify with that waterfall and wish to make a difference in caring will feel good in realizing that they are adding layers upon layers of peace, even if by civil disobedience, to an enlightened world.

The peace community of Kansas City offered points of light when five peacemakers crossed the line protesting nuclear weapons on Memorial Day 2018. Lu Mountenay, Tom Fox, Sunny Jordan Hamrick, Henry Stoever, and Brian Terrell went to trial, but because the prosecution's sole witness failed to appear in court, the case was dismissed. This is an example of one layer of peacemakers, with more to come next Memorial Day. As insignificant as this may seem, this is where civil disobedience makes a difference.

Ant X was recalling a dream he had the other night that came from deep within as we were casually talking about what "Thousand Points of Light" means to us. Scaling high on this peak and surveying the valley, he saw a mass of ants marching below in a monstrous circle as if they were going to war as if a huge blanket was pulsating up and down in ripples of cascading waves. Suddenly the ants were climbing on each other, hiking each one on top the other to form a huge boot that stomped on a mass of ants, squishing them into the mud when a tsunami-like tornado pushed a sludge of ants down this flue into the side of the mountain out the other end.

Only a mass genocide could be more violent. The ants were swirling around so fast, they wound up in a conflagration, sucked up in a consuming bonfire. They were leaves of ash flung into the heavens to become "points of light," spread everywhere to fill up the skies as far as one could see.

"What did that mean to you?"

"Well, it was just beautiful," Ant X passionately shared. "But it probably was as good of an explanation for the disappearance of ants in mass extermination as anything, or for that matter, the extinction of humanity, layers upon layers without noticing any reason for their elimination."

I pondered, "How honest is it if you just say it is a mystery? Things sometime just happen. Gone, insignificantly."

"Well, if one ends up as a point of light, that's not so bad," said Ant X, "like glistening in a winter fest."

Figment of Imagination

Art of Man of La Mancha

I LOVE EVERYTHING ABOUT the story "Man of La Mancha." I love listening to YouTube and hearing the many renditions of "The Impossible Dream," even the way Jim Nabors comes awkwardly out on stage in the persona of Gomer Pyle and surprises everyone with his powerful voice. So many voices have given us hope with this song. I am so taken with this story that I mentioned it in a sermon. I love the phrases by Joe Darion that raise the spirit to new heights: "to dream the impossible dream, to fight the unbeatable foe, to reach the unreachable star, This is my quest . . . to live in the world as it is traversed by man as he ought to be." The song is first sung by Don Quixote in response to Dulcinea's question about what he means by "following the quest."

"Just to be inspired by a quest is good enough for me," I added.

"You know, too many give up early," Ant X said, for some small talk.

The picture on my wall shows an ink drawing of Don Quixote de la Mancha on a horse Rocinante with his friend, Sancho Panza, ready to take on the world even if it means fighting windmills. The local paper in a front page picture September 7, 2013, showed peacemakers (me and another gentle soul, Christian Brother Louis Rodemann) carrying a door marked, "Open the Door to a Nuclear Weapons Free World." In the story, the city prosecutor was quoted as saying, "these people seem to be tilting at windmills" in resisting the new nuclear weapons plant. We were only mad knights who in our awkwardness tried to set things right and in doing so bring some joy to others.

"I keep thinking of fifty years ago when Robert Kennedy was assassinated and thus hope was dashed for our Man of La Mancha," I told the Ant. "Starting with John Fitzgerald Kennedy in 1963 and then losing MLK in 1968, we lost our innocence and a hope in the way 'things could have been.'

"I didn't think we could live through such a dark time, but here we are at another juncture of darkness," I said despondently. "The 'prez of chaos' is destroying this country now that he can select toxic candidates for Supreme Court judge.

"We seem to have reached a low point on the shortest day of the year, December 21, 2018, when the 'prez of chaos' allowed the government to shut down because the opposition party did not fund his wall."

"Could anyone have prevented this?" asked Ant X, shuffling his antennae up and down.

"Congress tried, but the President insisted that he needed the wall for national security with a price tag of five billion dollars." I responded.

Ant X quickly spoke up, "Why was the wall so important?"

"It appeared to be something visible, something solid," I reflected. "Actually, it was symbolic of this administration bringing a divide that would keep people out."

"Did we finally come full circle in wiping out anything that looked progressive and represented the hard work of a previous administration caring for the vulnerable?" asked the Ant, agreeing with me.

"This was a continuation of the end in a dark period of a nation's history," I said, shaking my head in disbelief.

"I have a premonition," declared Ant X.

"What's that? I inquired.

"Often the divide is straight down the middle, but the old ways are going to be replaced by something better!" noted Ant X, slashing his right antenna across his thorax and then straight ahead."

"I hope so."

"There is always light behind the shadows," the Ant calmly said.

I asked, "Which side has the truth? Fear or Love? Inertia or Progress? Destruction or Life? Which will set you free?"

Ant X looked puzzlingly optimistic, for some reason.

"I didn't want to call this book a book of darkness although it feels that way," I said, speculating on what might have been.

Ant X asked, "Why not?"

"Because life is more complicated than that," I said with my eyebrows raised.

"What do you mean?

"There is ambiguity in the opposites," I said. "Life is mixed up in the light and an awareness of darkness in all of us, shadows if you will, or hope in the darkest of days."

"You are just afraid to succumb to complete darkness," said the Ant. "Why does darkness seem to come before light?"

"I just want to believe in hope eventually," I said, "even though this nation is being attacked by an aggressive cancer cell."

I settle deeper in the beanbag, squinting my eyes but peeking out enough to let in some light. My darkness subdues me in a terror about what the Trump world will surprise us with next, but then he goes to Singapore and does away with "war games," which sets up a tizzy with the military but may end the Korean war. We never know how long these handshakes last.

"Only 'the Shadow' knows," Ant X peeps up creepily, whispering longingly.

What this bigger picture means to me is "flights of fancy." I have used the metaphor of ants to draw attention to our vulnerability and our insignificance when millions meet their end without a snicker or a nod of recognition. In other words, many are barely noticed and leave life without even a grave marker. An individual may not even be given a name that is his or her very own. I don't have a good answer for that, just sadness amongst my thinking friends.

My imagination goes wild when thinking about the reproduction of ants, which has certainly been the case with Ant X. I know I treated him as a unique individual when most of the time ants work as social beings. Most ants produce a new generation each year during a breeding period when it is hot in late spring, when females and winged males take a nuptial flight. Males take flight before the females, so I learn from Wikipedia, to find visual cues such as a tree for a landmark to direct other males to find the future nest. They secrete a mating pheromone that females follow. It is noted that males mount females in the air but usually the union takes place in the ground. Depending on the type of ant, some females have more than one mate to begin a colony, where they break off their wings and begin to care for the eggs. Work begins early to enlarge the nest and forage for food.

Here's what happened with me and the Ant. Sex is a powerful pull that needs channeling. Ant X took off without even having time to say good-bye.

I'll miss him.

I turn quietly sad, not demonstratively emotional, just incomplete and alone, until I can give myself permission to go on.

I find myself thinking about him when I listen to the waterfall by the Gazebo, not just as a friend but as someone I could dialogue with about insignificance. He made his mark but he was one of a million, hardly noticeable in the whole scheme of things. When this author stops writing this narrative and the book gathers dust on the bookshelves of life, who will notice except in the memory of our subconscious?

You might say that this book is another WOT (Waste Of Time) experience, but if you see it as part of leisure . . . well, it is as it is, and at least I enjoyed some of it. If I find myself in a thinking seminar I might say, "There is no such thing as a wasted life in leisure."

Thus Ant X left as a figment of my imagination, as so many things come and go. We had great times together. We learned to live in the moment. And now, we turn to different moments. The new moments will bring new friends or maybe nothing. Maybe the memories will fondly linger, maybe not.

Final Merging

So, Ant X helped me identify my attachments to images on the wall but he left about the time I needed to discover their insignificance. A spiritual connection was however made—a revelation of the X factor, a sign of some sense of the spirit that allows us to be significantly authentic.

The "X" factor was always a reminder of Ant X. Call it what you will, it was always a reference to the Christ, a sense of Spirit, a way to talk about a uniting energy as a sustaining movement from alpha to omega, from beginning to end, as a build-up of layers—ant-by-ant, human-by-human, creation-by-creation. When I think about marriage with Toni my love, we have a symbol embedded in our rings, *KRONI*, referring to Ron and Toni connected to ChiRho meaning a Christ recognition merging in the ripeness of time. That uniting principle encompasses the intimacy of our friends and family united in community, connected in Communion, layered as "multi-cute" Ant X's, as insignificant as that may seem, taking on a part of the whole, suffering when others suffer and working for peace.

I surmised, "The way I see it, I no longer needed Ant X when I found my own voice. I merged as one, more authentic, less uncertain."

Well, let's face it. We are insignificant, like ants. And when we can face it humbly we have a better chance to be authentic. We will stack up better for our humility than for how great we are. Still, still, we have participated in the human enterprise even if we don't write a book that will soon be forgotten, although this one will go to the grandkids if the world I protested for is still around. I hope it is, because my children and all those attached were a small gift of my contribution.

I come to the end not knowing when it will end. How could it get any better than this? A flight of fancy and a moment with the Queen! How will it get worse than this? All who deny climate change and vote for destructive leadership!

Yet it was better in the end. The tide changed faster than night turns to day. The season of winter on February 27, 2019 gave way to springtime, fresh and honest. The testimony of inside lawyer Michael Cohen, however discredited, pushed back on the lies of a Trump administration, reversing a checkered past of hush money to porn stars, hacked E-mails damaging Clinton's campaign and insight on Russian intervention in the election. Unbelievable. Complicit in this stream of destruction were the voters who were misled in their cult-like loyalty to the "Prez of chaos." In the midterm election of 2018 a bold, bigger bang of light sprinkled shadows of peace across a span representing decades of divide. It felt like progress in the shifting shadows.

Turning on and off the lamp above the beanbag in the corner of the Room, I'm taking it all in, glad to be alive and see late shadows spread across the floor. It's unsettling and complicated to take in a wavy mixture of hope and disappointment. I am also okay to sit in darkness with my eyes closed. I knew at the time that my fellow humans were unknowingly out to destroy this country. Not the people I personally know but some people in higher places. I would like to see the people I touched continue what we set forth. From my corner advantage point, from my beanbag that enters my Shalom zone, my story comes to the end of Quadrant IV that comfortably hugs me now on all four sides.

A final dimension is the glass doorway with a modern-day picture of Jesus overlooking the city, with the word "Peace." I think I prefer an expansive metaphor in the *Asteroides* painting by Leonardo Niermann, which offers a feeling of free fall into a myriad of stars much like visiting Space Mountain at the Epcot Center, and then perhaps being cushioned by a safety net of a mattress of ants.

It was like Ant X calling from far away, "What a way to go!"

The Rising

Sometimes I think when it is my time, I might cast a vision of a singled-layered quilt, beautifully woven by family member Alice Brooks, who created a patchwork of interesting stories, some more significant than others, thinly stacked in humanity's closet but thrown to the cosmic winds as if I were sailing around the world. It doesn't matter that that's a bit nonsensical, but do you know what I mean? I thought I would come off this journey discovering something spectacular for my pride, but instead I'm only feeling like a mere ant. Other times I am certain that I will have a glimpse of the body, creating shadows, both at the bottom then at the top, from the stained-glass window called *The Rising* because it expresses pure exuberance. Ahh, herein lies significance—rare and memorable. Instead, mostly I'm lost in the shadows.

I go to my beanbag for solace. I turn on the tiny light spreading shadows, hear some gentle music and find hope in the illusive shadows of Peace.

Appendix

ABOUT THE COVER PICTURE

The Rising by Ed Johnson of Salem, Oregon, purchased on August 19, 1987, when it caught my eye in a coastal Seaside, Oregon, shop. One of those "Aha" moments. Traces of the artist in Salem are unknown to the author but this work is in the personal art collection of Ron and Toni Faust.

ABOUT THE ROOM

This Study is a collection of a lifetime of mementoes with many Sabbath stories of friends, academic work, and peacemaking activities.

About the Author

Ronald L. Faust, B.Th., M.Div., D.Min. CFLE

REV. DR. RON FAUST works with peace, justice and ecology groups such as PeaceWorks and Disciples Peace Fellowship. He received a Doctorate from DREW University in Madison, New Jersey, and

About the Author

an M.Div. from Christian Theological Seminary in Indianapolis. He was born and attended Northwest Christian College (NCU) in Eugene, Oregon. At the center of his circle of love are his wife, Toni; their children, Jeremy and Tuesday; and five grandchildren: Isaac, Claira, Eleanor, Elsie and Paloma. He likes to create poetry under his Gazebo or out on his sailboat, Sabbatical II.

Books by the Author

Volume 1: *Prophetic Poetry: A Holy Agitation for Peace, Justice, and Passion* from www.wipfandstock.com or call 541-344-1528

This collection of poetry expands the range of social justice issues and becomes a good daily meditation source.

Volume 2: *Prophetic Poetry: A Holy Occasion for Peace, Justice, and Ecology* from www.smashwords.com or Amazon.com

The poems offer resistance to Drones and nuclear weapons while introducing key themes to ethical issues.

Volume 3: *Prophetic Poetry: A Holy Occasion for Openness, Authenticity, and Love* from www.smashwords.com

This poetry gives us prophetic alerts to things that matter while urging us "to smooth out the hard edges in the process of authentic living."

Volume 4: *POEMS for Lonely Prophets* from Green Ivy Publishing

These occasional poems continue commenting on social injustices and demonstrate that unpopular prophets discern the destructiveness of some mainstream thinking.

GAPS by pseudonym Mac Keyes from Xlibris.com

A fictional account follows Blake across Missouri, Swaziland and Iraq as he joins a contest to unlock confusion about spiritual, sexual and family values.

Books by the Author

GRAND PARENTING for Compassion and Peace by Ronald L. Faust and Toni B. Faust from Smashwords.com

This nonfictional account offers tips for raising healthy, adjusted children and explores the mentoring role that Grandparents play in a world of compassion and peace.

Five Faces of Love by pseudonym Mac Keyes from Amazon or Smashwords

This collection of love poems explores the five dimensions of love in its lustiness, deep friendships, taking care of others, correcting injustices and as a form of peace.

A Room Full of Shadows from Ron Faust and Wipf and Stock

The author takes a journey around his Room in dialogue with an ant whose life seems insignificant. The quizzical book starts out, "Sometimes I feel like an ant." The author discovers that we all end up with this feeling no matter how many stories we can tell or whenever we try to beat death. This book is a combination of stories about protests, the dynamics of music and art, plus the work of a peacemaker.

www.ingramcontent.com/pod-product-compliance
Lightning Source LLC
Chambersburg PA
CBHW071445150426
43191CB00008B/1247